北京的胡同是中国惟一的

也是世界惟一的

北京胡同里有数不尽的好建筑

处处都有人文故事

撒满了文物古迹

东冠英胡同的春天　　Dongguanying(East Guangin) Hutong in spring

......

胡同的记忆，

就是北京悠久历史的传承，

就是浓郁京味文化的浸润，

也是人们怀旧情感的自然流露

和对生身故土的热切依恋。

从车流如潮的神州第一街到幽深曲折的小胡同；

从斑驳残破的砖墙到起伏似灰色波浪的四合院房脊；

还有胡同中的阴晴雨雪、

风晨月夕、年节习俗、四季变化；

更有那生活在小胡同中、四合院里的

形形色色的北京人，

林林总总，蔚为大观

......

...The memory of Hutong

represents the inheritance of

long history of Beijing and strong

influence of culture of Beijing style.

Also, it awakens the reminiscences of the

past and fervent attachment to the hometown.

They start from the No.1 Boulevard in China to tran-

quil and winding alleys, the incomplete and bro-

ken brick walls to wavelike room ridge in

Siheyuan, various weathers, festivals and

customs, movement of four seasons,

and diversity of Beijingers living

in Hutong and Siheyuan ...

胡同的记忆

王文波／摄影

Recollections of Hutong

砖塔胡同 位于西城区中部的西四南大街西侧,因东口有万松老人塔而得名。这是一条自元代至今名称未变的古老胡同。据《日下旧闻考》载:"砖塔七级,高丈五尺,有石额曰万松老人塔。清乾隆十八年(1753年)奉敕修九级,仍旧制",今塔尚保存完好。鲁迅、老舍、张恨水均在此胡同住过。老舍在小说《离婚》中写道:"砖塔胡同,离电车站近,离市场近,而胡同里又比兵马司和丰盛胡同清静一些,比大院胡同整齐一些,最宜住家。"

Zhuanta (Brick Pagoda) Hutong is situated to the west of South Xisi Street in the middle of Xicheng District. The name came from the brick pagoda of Wansong Laoren (Ten-Thousand-Pine Old Man) at the eastern entrance to the hutong, and has never been changed since the Yuan Dynasty. According to the *Rixia Jiuwen Kao* (*Study on Old Stories of the Capital*): " The 7-storey brick pagoda was 1 *zhang* and 5 *chi* high (roughly equaling to 5 meters). Its stone horizontal inscribed board bearing the name of pagoda. In 1753, the 18th year of Qing Emperor Qianlong's reign, it was reconstructed to be a 9-storey structure in accordance with the original model." The tower still remains intact till now. Lu Xun, Lao She and Zhang Henshui once lived in this hutong. Lao She even wrote in his novel *The Divorce*, "Zhuanta Hutong is not far away from the tram stop and market. Furthermore, it is more tranquil than Bingmasi (literally, Soldiers and Horses Department) Hutong and Fengsheng (Rich) Hutong, trimmer and orderlier than Dayuan (Big Courtyard) Hutong. It is an ideal place for the residence."

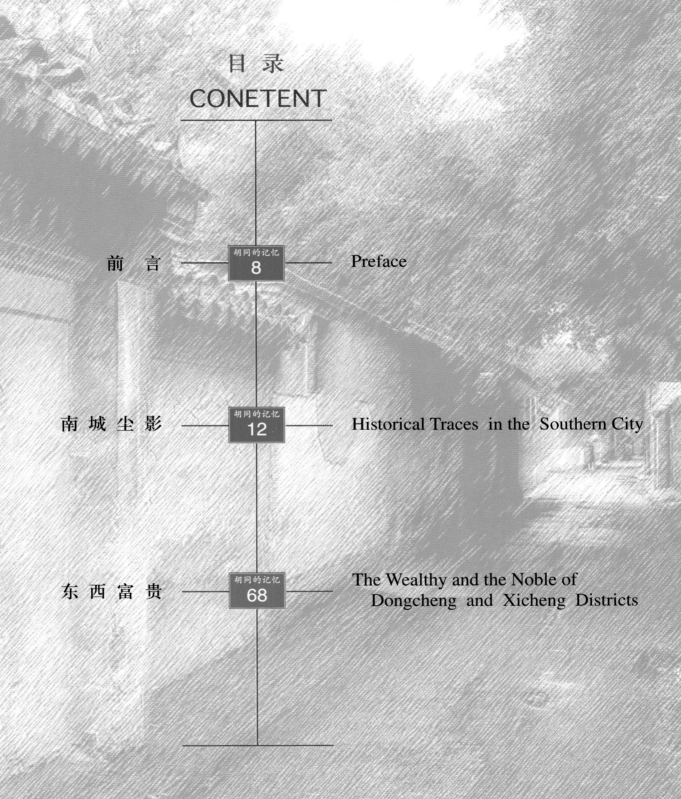

目 录
CONETENT

前　言

"有名的胡同三千六，没名的胡同如牛毛"，这是老北京人形容京城胡同众多的俗语。北京这个有着三千多年建城史和八百多年建都史的古老城市中，那纵横交错、历尽沧桑的胡同与大气磅礴、金碧辉煌的皇宫相互辉映，构成了京城的万千气象。然而，代表贵族建筑的紫禁城及皇家园林仅占古都北京的五分之一，代表平民文化的胡同、四合院则有着更为广大的地域，北京的精髓也隐藏于深巷广衢之中。

说起胡同的称呼，要比北京的名称早上一百多年。北京古称蓟、燕，唐代为幽州，辽称南京，金为中都，到元大都之时，开始按城市规划有了"衖通"（胡同）之称，并按"胡同"宽6步（约合9．3米）、小街（火巷）宽12步（约合18．6米）、大街宽24步（约合37．2米）的规定动工兴建。元代熊梦祥著的《析津志》中记载大都城内有"三百八十四火巷，二十九胡同"，此时为元大都初建成时的至元十三年（1276年）。此后，直到1403年，明朝的永乐皇帝迁都京师始将"北平"改称为"北京"，这样算来胡同的称号要比北京的名称早上127年。

北京胡同的格局和建置则是从唐代的幽州城历经辽、金、元、明、清诸朝而逐渐完善起来的。据《辽史·地理志》描述：辽南京位于现在北京城西南方宣武区的西部，城呈长方形，周长18公里，基本上沿用的是唐代幽州城的原有建置，只是把城墙重加修筑，全城有8个城门，城内交通道路呈井字型，南北和东西方向各有主干道2条，这4条主干道将全城划分为9大区域。西南区域为宫城占地，其他区域内各有若干条次干道与主干道相连，城中有26个坊，坊内有府第、寺庙、民居等。今日的北线阁胡同地处辽南京城北的通天门内，是当时最繁华的街道。

金中都是在辽南京的基础上，以宋代汴京（开封）为范本，"役民八十万，兵夫四十万"改、扩建成的。金中都的城垣位置在今日地图上大略为：东南城角在今永定门火车站西南的四路通；东北城角在今宣武门内的翠花街；西北城角在今中华世纪坛南边的羊坊店、黄亭子；西南城角在今丰台区凤凰嘴村。城南的丰宜门为纵贯全城南北的中轴线南端，它穿过皇城往北直达通玄门，是中都城平面布局的中枢。丰宜门西边为端礼门，北对会城门……全城十二个城门引申相通的街衢，今天仍依稀可辨。金中都的改、扩建，结束了我国历史上唐宋之时的城市坊巷结构，由封闭型改为开放型的街市，这在我国城市发展史上有重要意义，对于元、明、清城市格局的建设也有示范和参考作用。

元大都城选址在金中都城东北郊外，是按照《周礼·考工记》的规划原则并结合当地实际情况设计兴建的。其东西界即为现在北京内城东、西城垣，南界约在今天的东、西长安街一线；北界在今北三环路北侧的土城。大都城的每一座城门内都有一条笔直的干道，连同顺城街在内共有九条纵横交错的干道。今天的东四南北大街，西四南北大街，西直门内大街以及东四北头条到十四条都是昔日元大都的旧街道，它为今日北京城奠定了基础。

公元1368年，朱元璋的大将军徐达，率领军队攻占元大都，命令指挥华云龙"经理元故都，新筑城垣"把元大都的北墙南移至今日安定门、德胜门一线。永乐十七年（1419年），明成祖朱棣定都北京之后，将北京城南垣移到今前三门一线。明嘉靖年间增修北京外城，使前门外商业活动日益活跃，人口日渐稠密，又出现了许多新居民区和新的街道。

清代北京的街巷胡同虽然比明代大为增加（明代有街巷胡同1170条，直接称为胡同的有459条；清代《京师坊巷志稿》记有街巷胡同2077条，直接称为胡同的有978条），但有相当一部分是原有胡同的扩大与发展（如某胡同的拓展与沿伸），有的仅为局部调整（如一条长巷分割为两至三段，成为两、三条胡同），从整体而言，清代北京街巷胡同与明代格局基本相同。

现在北京人说的胡同是泛指北京的大街小巷，摆在您面前的这本画册，题名为《胡同的记忆》，它记录、拍摄的也是京城中的大马路、小胡同，以及构成胡同的最基本元素——四合院及大小院落（大宅门、大杂院、三合院等）。胡同的记忆，实际上就是北京悠久历史的传承，就是浓郁京味文化的浸润，也是人们怀旧情感的自然流露和对生身故土的热切依恋。摄影家王文波先生正是摸准了胡同的脉搏，参透了胡同的文化底蕴，从20世纪70年代初到2005年，历时三十余年，栉风沐雨，用他那平实的摄影风格，拍下了数百条胡同的倩影，记下了历史的变迁、时代的风貌。从车流如潮的神州第一街到幽深曲折的小胡同；从斑驳残破的砖墙到起伏似灰色波浪的四合院房脊；还有胡同中的阴晴雨雪、风晨月夕、年节习俗、四季变化；更有那生活在小胡同中、四合院里的形形色色的北京人，林林总总，蔚为大观，构成了这册集旅游、欣赏、收藏为一体的精美画册。

有人曾说：如果把北京城比做一棵枝叶繁茂的千年古树，那么，胡同就是这棵大树的枝干；如果把北京城比做一个堂堂正正的奇伟男子，胡同就是一条隐伏于人体内的四通八达的血脉，有了它，北京的精气神才能贯通；如果把北京城比做一部情节复杂的长篇小说，那么，胡同就是一个个细节，有了它，这本书才会生动、传神、引人入胜。且让我们展开画册，读一读北京胡同这本大书的精彩细节，慢慢品味原汁原味的北京四合院风情，探寻古老北京胡同前进、变化的轨迹，在心中留下深沉的胡同记忆吧！

Preface

There is a common saying among old Beijingers that describes the huge amounts of Hutongs that " There are 3,600 major hutongs in Beijing while the minor ones as many as the hairs on an ox". Myriads of aged Hutongs intersect with each other, which are contrasting sharply with the majestic, imposing and splendid royal palaces. They represent the diverse charms of Beijing which has a history of more than 3,000 years as a city and over 800 years as a capital. However, the Forbidden City and royal gardens standing for the noble structures only account for one fifth of the whole Beijing; while Hutongs and Siheyuans (quadrangle) with characteristics of common people's life cover a larger area and the essences of Beijing's history are also hidden in these alleys.

The call of Hutong is more than 100 years earlier than the name of Beijing. Beijing was called Ji and Yan in ancient China, and Youzhou in Tang Dynasty, Nanjing in Liao Dynasty, Zhongdu in Jin Dynasty. When it became the capital of Yuan Dynasty, the word of "Xiangtong" (lane, or Hutong) was begun to be used. According to the city planning of the Yuan Dynasty, the width of a hutong should be six paces (about 9.3 meters), while a side street or (also known as huoxiang) 12 paces (about 18.6 meters), and that of an avenue should be 24 paces (about 37.2 meters). "There were 384 huoxiangs and 29 hutongs in the Dadu (Great Capital) of the Yuan Dynasty", as said by Xiong Mengxiang, a scholar of the Yuan, on the *Xi Jin Zhi* (*Analytic Records of Beijing*) in 1276 (the 13th year under reign title of Zhiyuan) when the construction of Great Capital was just finished. Yet it was in 1403 when the Ming emperor Yongle moved capital that the city got its present name: Beijing, instead of Beiping. So the call of Hutong was 127 years earlier than the name of Beijing.

The layout and arrangement of Hutong in Beijing, starting from the Youzhou of Tang, were gradually improved in such successive feudal dynasties as Liao, Jin, Yuan, Ming and Qing. As stated in *Dili Zhi of Liao Shi* (*Geographical Records of the History of Liao Dynasty*): the Nanjing of Liao Dynasty was situated in west of Xuanwu District of present Beijing. The whole city, rectangle in shape and 18 kilometers in circumference, mostly followed the layout of Youzhou in Tang Dynasty, except that the city walls were reconstructed. There were 8 city gates on the wall in total. There were 2 north-south arteries and 2 east-west arteries intersected each other like the Chinese character " 井 ", dividing the city into 9 rectangular blocks. The block in the southwest was allocated for the royal palaces. The other 8 blocks were subdivided by several minor roads connecting the arteries into 26 fangs, in which mansions, temples and residences of common people were established. The current Beixiange (literally North Thread Tower, mispronunciation of Corner Tower

of Yan) Hutong was situated inside the Yongtian Gate in Nanjing City of Liao Dynasty. It used to be the most bustling street at that time.

Zhongdu (Middle Capital) of Jin Dynasty was based on the Nanjing City of Liao Dynasty and followed the example of Bianjing (today's Kaifeng City in Henan Province) of Song Dynasty. It was reconstructed and expanded with the employment of 800,000 civilians and 400,000 soldiers. The outline of Zhongdu in the current map is as follows: the southeastern corner of the city is situated at the Silutong Area to the southwest of Yongding Gate Railway Station; the northeastern corner is on the Cuihua Street inside Xuanwu Gate; the northwestern corner is on the Yangfangdian and Huangtingzi to the south of China Millennium Monument; the southwestern corner is on today's Fenghuangzui Village in Fengtai District. Fengyi Gate served as the southern end of the south-north central axes passing through the city, which extended through the royal city till Tongxuan Gate supposed to be the backbone of the plane layout of Zhongdu. A total of 12 city gates were built in matching pairs and facing each other at either side, such as the Duanli Gate to the west of Fengyi Gate facing the Huicheng Gate in the north. The streets linked up these 12 gates could be distinguished vaguely even in today. The reconstruction and expansion of Zhongdu brought an end to the layout of lanes and alleys in Tang and Song dynasties. Beijing began to develop from an isolated city into an open one, which represented an important stage of city development in Chinese history as well as served as a perfect model for the city pattern in Yuan, Ming and Qing dynasties.

The northeastern suburbs of Zhongdu of Jin Dynasty were selected as the location of Dadu of Yuan Dynasty. It was designed and constructed in line with the layout principles stated in the *Kaogong Ji of Zhou Li* (*Engineering Research of the Ritual of Zhou*) and local situations. The eastern and western boundaries are the ruins of eastern and western walls of Inner City of Beijing in present day; the southern boundary is located roughly along today's Eastern and Western Chang'an (Eternal Peace) Boulevard; while the northern boundary is located at today's Tucheng, north to the Northern 3rd Ring Road. A straight main road was built inside each city gate. Therefore, there were 9 main roads along with Shuncheng Street intersecting with each other. In nowadays, the South and North Dongsi streets, South and North Xisi streets, Xizhimennei Street and the streets from the 1st North Hutong to 14th North Hutong of Dongsi in Beijing used to be the roads of Dadu of Yuan Dynasty. Those ancient roads laid the foundation for today's Beijing.

In 1368, Xu Da, the general of Zhu Yuanzhang, seized Dadu by force. After the subjection, Xu Da ordered the Commander Hua Yunlong to administer the former capital city of Yuan and rebuild city walls. Hereafter, the northern section of the city wall was moved southward to the current Anding Gate and Dengsheng Gate. In 1419 (the 17th year of Ming Emperor Yongle's reign) when Zhu Di (also known as Chengzu of Ming) moved capital to Beijing, the southern city wall was shifted to south, along today's Qiansanmen (Front Three Gates) Street. During the reign of Ming Emperor Jiajing, the Outer City wall of Beijing was added. More and more businesses swarmed outside Qianmen Gate and population began to swell. Many new residence areas and streets emerged.

Compared with the number of alleys and lanes in Ming Dynasty, the number in Qing Dynasty increased considerably (There were 1,170 streets, alleys and lanes in Beijing during the Ming, and 459 of them were called Hutong directly; as stated described in the *Jingshi Fangxiang Zhigao*, or *Records of Lane and Alley in Capital*, there were 2,077 streets, alleys and lanes during the Qing, and 978 of them were called Hutong directly.). However, a quite number of the streets, alleys and lanes were expanded or developed on basis of the former ones (for example, a further development or extension of some hutongs), and some were rearranged (for example, a long alley was divided into two or three sections, forming two or three new hutongs). Generally speaking, the layout of streets, alley and lane in Qing Dynasty almost copied that in Ming Dynasty.

The term Hutong mentioned frequently by Beijingers refers to the major streets and little lanes or alleys in general. This picture album before you is titled as the *Recollections of Hutong*, which records major roads and little hutongs in Beijing, as well as Siheyuan and various courtyards (including Dazhaimen, Dazayuan and Sanheyuan) — the basic fabrics of Hutong. The memory of Hutong represents the inheritance of long history of Beijing and strong influence of culture of Beijing style. Also, it awakens the reminiscences of the past and fervent attachment to the hometown. It was photographer Mr. Wang Wenbo that grasped the development trend and cultural indications of Hutong. With great efforts, he took large numbers of beautiful pictures of thousands of Hutongs in simple and plain photographic style from the 1970s to the year of 2005, a spanning of more than 30 years. These pictures have recorded the variances of history and new phenomenon in the modern age. From the bustling No.1 Street in China to tranquil and winding alleys, from the incomplete and broken brick walls to wavelike room ridges in Siheyuan, these pictures showcase hutongs' distinctive charms in various weathers, as well as lives, festivals and customs of diverse Beijingers living in Hutong and Siheyuan. All these constitute an enchanting picture album which presents a splendid sight of Beijing. It can serve as your tour guide, for your appreciation and collection.

Someone once said: If Beijing city is compared to an ancient tree of over 1,000 years, the Hutongs are the branches; if Beijing is compared to an excellent man of integrity, the Hutongs are the veins spreading through the whole body whereby Beijing's spirits can be revealed; if Beijing is compared to a complicated novel, the Hutongs represent the details whereby this book is lifelike, vivid and appealing. Now, let's open this picture album and read about the details of Hutongs in Beijing. And we will have a taste of original life in Siheyuan and explore developments and changes of ancient Hutongs in Beijing. We will have deep recollection of Hutongs.

南城尘影

北京城的城市建置由紫禁城、皇城、内城和外城这大圈圈套小圈圈的四座城池组成，原内城、外城形同"凸"字型。这城南就是指内城南边，即前三门（正阳门、崇文门、宣武门）南边的外城，俗称南城帽的范围，也就是今日崇文和宣武两区。

宣武区是北京城的发祥地，《北京建城记碑》中载："北京城区建城之始则在蓟，蓟之中心在今宣武区，其地承先启后，源远流长立石为记，永志不忘……"今日宣武区的胡同历史可上溯至唐、辽、金、元、明、清各朝。在这块古老的地域内，有唐朝巨刹法源寺及幽州街巷遗踪；有辽代的天宁寺宝塔，金代修建的莲花池苑；有闻名遐迩的繁华街市大栅栏，古色古香的琉璃厂。在那众多会馆的古槐深处、紫藤架边、灯火樽前、海棠花下，曾经有无数文人雅集、诗酒流连，诞生过那么多瑰词丽句、巨制鸿篇，形成了集皇家文化、士人文化、民俗文化、商业文化、民族文化、宗教文化、梨园文化等于一身的丰富内涵，成为北京文化的历史缩影，发出了令人眩目的光彩。

自明朝正统二年(1437年)，将内城南部三门东侧的文明门改为崇文门后，"崇文"之称已有560余年。岁月沧桑，如今天坛、袁崇焕祠、明城墙遗址、正阳门城楼等105处文物遗存，如一颗颗明珠在崇文大地熠熠生辉，它们是历史的财富，崇文的骄傲。

今天，让我们且随同王文波先生的摄影镜头，在那一处处早已变了容颜的冷僻胡同、荒芜院落中访古探幽，从几乎泯灭的淡痕中寻觅千年旧迹，从古老的南城尘影和新时代的高楼大厦中见证历史的演进。

Historical Traces in the Southern City

The layout of Beijing consisted of four cities — the Forbidden City, Royal City, Inner City and Outer City — in form of concentric rings. The original Outer City was shaped like the Chinese character " 凸 ". The southern city refers to the area south to the Inner City, namely the Outer City outside the Qiansanmen (Zhengyang Gate, Chongwen Gate and Xuanwu Gate). The Outer City usually called Nanchengmao (Cap of Southern City) includes the current Chongwen and Xuanwu districts.

Xuanwu District is the cradle of Beijing City. According to the statement in the *Records of Construction of Beijing* carved on stele: "The construction of Beijing city originated from Ji and the center of Ji was just situated in the current Xuanwu District. This location of a long history inherited the past and ushered in the future. Here stands the stele for the ever-lasting memory". The Hutongs in this district could be traced back to Tang, Liao, Jin, Yuan, Ming and Qing dynasties. Within this ancient area, there stands eminent Fayuan (Origin of Dharma) Temple and many traces of alleys and lanes from You Zhou of Tang Dynasty. Additionally, there are pagoda in the Tianning (Heavenly Peace) Temple of Liao Dynasty, Lianhuachi (Lotus-Flower Pond) Garden built in Jin Dynasty, well-known Dazhalan (Great Fence) Street and Liulichang (Glazed Tile Plant) Street with antique flavors. Numerous scholars created myriads of marvelous verses and magnificent works in guild halls hidden among aged Chinese scholar-trees and wisteria. This district is a hub of royal culture, literati and officialdom culture, folk culture, business culture, national culture, religious culture and Beijing Opera culture. It is seen as the epitome of cultures in Beijing and presents impressive splendor.

The name of Chongwen enjoys a history of over 560 years since the Wenming Gate, one of the three southern gates of the Inner City, was re-named as Chongwen Gate in 1437, the 2nd year of Ming Emperor Zhengtong's reign. Many cultural relics, including the Temple of Heaven, Ancestral Temple of Yuan Chonghuan, relics of the Ming city wall and the tower of Zhengyang Gate, are of historic values and pride of Chongwen District. Also, they like shining pearls enhance the fame of the district.

Now, the photos by Mr. Wang Wenbo will guide us to explore the historic sites that are almost forgotten by people through the remote alleys and deserted yards that have underwent changes, and to witness the historical developments among the traces of ancient southern city and modern skyscrapers.

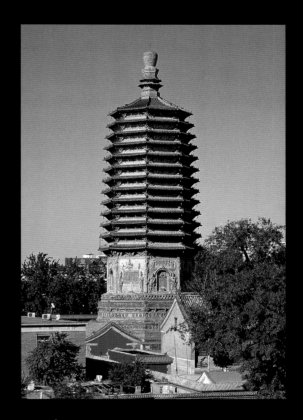

天宁寺塔 是北京城区现存最古老的地上建筑，始建于辽代大康九年（1083年），已巍然挺立九百余年。此塔高达57.8米，为八角十三层密檐式实心砖塔。塔的基座分为两层分别雕有狮头及浮雕坐佛。塔身四面设有半圆形券门，门两边雕有金刚力士、菩萨及云龙图案，造型生动，栩栩如生。十三层塔檐逐层收减，呈现出丰富有力的卷刹，造型挺拔俊美。

Pagoda of Tianning Temple is the oldest structure on the ground extant in Beijing proper. It was first constructed in 1083, the 9th year under the reign title of Dakang of the Liao Dynasty. This imposing and stately pagoda has stood there for over 900 years. The solid octagonal brick pagoda, 57.8 meters tall, has 13 storeys. Patterns of lion head and sitting Buddha were carved on the two-level base respectively. Arched doors are carved on the four sides of the pagoda, together with vivid and exquisite relief patterns of guardian warriors, Bodhisattvas and dragons flying in clouds. The 13 eaves of the tall and straight pagoda are constructed as to taper little by little, demonstrating the powerful rolling effect.

法源寺 位于宣武区中部,这是北京城内现存历史最久的名刹。它始建于唐贞观十九年(645年),是唐太宗李世民为追念东征阵亡将士而修建的,初名悯忠寺。安史之乱时,安禄山、史思明分别在寺的东南隅和西南隅各建塔一座,后毁于火灾。宋、元、明、清历朝对该寺曾有修葺改造,清雍正十二年(1734年)重修后更名为法源寺。这座古老的寺院自唐迄今,寺址未变,是考察唐幽州城址的重要依据。寺周围的街巷幽深、宁静,为今人留下了悠远的胡同记忆。

Fayuan Temple is situated in the center of Xuanwu District. It is the oldest existing temple in Beijing proper. It was first built in 645, the 19th year under reign title of Zhenguan, by order of Emperor Taizong, named Li Shimin, of the Tang Dynasty to commemorate his generals and soldiers who died in the battle against the northern State of Liao. At the time it was called Minzhong Temple (Temple in Memory of the Loyal). During the Rebellions of An Lushan and Shi Siming, the two generals constructed one tower in the southeast corner and southwest corner respectively, both of which were burned down later. The temple experienced several renovations during Song, Yuan, Ming and Qing dynasties, and in 1734, the 12th year of Qing Emperor Yongzheng's reign, it got its present name after a reconstruction. The location of this ancient temple has never been changed since Tang Dynasty, providing convincingly witness to the study on the location of Youzhou of Tang. The alleys surrounding the temple are deep and serene, which remind tourists of long-standing history of the Hutong.

大殿内整洁肃穆。
The main hall is tidy and solemn.

法源寺南(前)街 绿树掩映着红色山门、高大影壁,一对古朴的石狮列于街北的庙门前,使古老的胡同呈现出雄浑的气象。

South Fayuan Temple Street
The trees shroud the red gate and high screen wall. A pair of simple-carved stone lions stands in front of the gate of the temple to the north of the street, making the whole alley take on a vigorous and firm look.

西砖胡同 在法源寺东侧，明代曾称砖儿胡同，清末始称西砖胡同。北京的四大名医之一施今墨先生曾在胡同中段路东一宅院中创办华北国医学院，培养了一批中医人才。

Xizhuan (Western Brick) **Hutong** is situated to the east of Fayuan Temple. It used to be called Zhuaner (Bricks) Hutong in Ming Dynasty and got its present name in the end of Qing Dynasty. Mr. Shi Jinmo, one of the four most famous doctors in Beijing, once set up North China School of Traditional Chinese Medicine in a courtyard located east of the middle section of this alley and trained many professionals of traditional Chinese medicine.

烂缦胡同 位于法源寺东部、南横街北侧。这里曾是辽南京城东墙外的护城河。明朝初年河水干涸形成胡同，初称烂面胡同、懒眠胡同，清末改称烂缦胡同。此巷中有湖南、浙江、济南会馆。清乾隆时湖广总督毕沅曾居此胡同中，著有《山海经新校注》等。胡同北部多商店铺面，有清华斋糕点铺及首饰楼等。

Lanman Hutong is situated to the east of Fayuan Temple and the north of Nanheng Street. This alley used to be the moat beside the eastern section of the city wall of Nanjing in Liao Dynasty. In the beginning of Ming Dynasty, the river was dried up to be a hutong, named Lanmian (Mashed Dough, or Lazy and Sleepy) Hutong at that time. It was called Lanman (Bright Colored) in the end of Qing Dynasty. Ther guild halls of Hunan, Zhejiang and Jinan were built in this lane. Bi Yuan, the governor of Hunan and Guangdong lived in this alley during the reign of Emperor Qianlong. He was the author of *Shan Hai Jing Xin Jiaozhu* (*New Commentaries on the Classics of Mountains and Seas*) and others. There were a number of stores and shops to the north of the alley, including Cake Store of Qinghuazhai and jewelry stores and so on.

（右页）烂缦胡同南口的一个四合院
(Right) A Siheyuan at the southern entrance to the Lanman Hutong

南横西街 位于法源寺南部,这是辽金时代皇城西门外唯一的横向街道,故称南横街。这条具有八百多年历史的胡同中,店铺林立、会馆毗连。胡同东口路北的怡园,曾为明代严嵩的别墅,清康熙朝大学士王崇简、王熙父子在此建别业;清末在此建粤东会馆,康有为、梁启超成立的保国会就设在这里。1912 年孙中山曾至此参加欢迎会。胡同西口有建于金代的圣安寺。

West Nanheng Street Located to the south of Fayuan Temple, West Nanheng (South Horizontal) Street was the only east-west street outside the west gate of the royal city during Liao and Jin dynasties. Stores stand in great numbers and guild halls adjoin each other in this hutong with a history of over 800 years. Yiyuan Garden (Garden of Pleasure), to the north of the eastern entrance to this hutong, was once the villa of Yan Song, a corrupt official of the Ming Dynasty. Wang Chongjian, grand secretary during the reign of Emperor Kangxi, and his son Wang Xi constructed their mansion here. The Yuedong Guild Hall was established on this location in the end of Qing Dynasty, and Kang Youwei and Liang Qichao set up the Baoguohui (a reforming organ) in the guild hall. In 1912, Dr. Sun Yat-sen also attended the welcome meeting here. There stands Sheng'an (Holy Peace) Temple built in Jin Dynasty at the western entrance to the hutong.

胡同中的老店铺（已拆除）
Aged stores in the hutong
(It no longer exists)

圣安寺遗迹

　　胡同西口的圣安寺，始建于金代天会至大定年间（1123–1189年），明代改称普济寺，清乾隆四十一年（1776年）重修复称圣安寺。现存山门及天王殿为清代建筑。

Relics of Sheng'an Temple

　　The relics of Sheng'an Temple is located to the western entrance of this alley. The temple was built between the reigns of Emperor Tianhui and Emperor Dading (1123-1189) of the Jin Dynasty. It was renamed as Puji (Universal Charity) Temple in Ming Dynasty. In 1776, the 41st year of Qing Emperor Qianlong's reign, the temple was reconstructed and renamed as Sheng'an Temple. The current gate and Tianwang (Heavenly King) Hall in the temple were built in Qing Dynasty.

南半截胡同 位于南横西街北侧,北有北半截胡同,因胡同长度仅为全部街巷之半而得名。胡同北路西有绍兴会馆,鲁迅先生曾在此居住七年多,创作了中国现代文学史上第一部白话短篇小说《狂人日记》。北半截胡同中的江苏会馆相传为明代严世藩别墅,其南有著名的广和居饭庄,为清末官吏、文人墨客、梨园子弟欢聚之处;维新派领袖谭嗣同等人于1899年曾在胡同中的浏阳会馆被捕遇难。

Nanbanjie (South Half) Hutong is located to the north of West Nanheng Street, adjacent to Beibanjie (North Half) Hutong in the north. The name came into being because its length is only half that of the whole street. There stands Shaoxing Guild Hall to the west of the northern section of this alley. Mr. Lu Xun had lived in the Guild Hall for over 7 years and created *A Madman's Diary*, the first short story written in a vernacular style in Chinese modern literature history. Jiangsu Guild Hall in Beibanjie Hutong was said to be the villa of Yan Shifan, son of Yan Song. To the south, there is the famous Guangheju Restaurant where was a gathering place for officials, scholars and opera players during the end of Qing Dynasty. Tan Sitong, the leader of ardent supporters of 1898 Reform Movement, and other colleagues were arrested in Liuyang Guild Hall in this hutong and later killed.

门墩
Gate piers

(右页)小雪后的南半截胡同与南横西街交汇处
(Right) The juncture of Nanbanjie Hutong and West Nanheng Street after mild snow

绍兴会馆

位于南半截胡同的绍兴会馆，鲁迅先生曾在此居住七年多。

Shaoxing Guild Hall

Shaoxing Guild Hall is situated in Nanbanjie Hutong, in which Mr. Lu Xun once lived for over 7 years.

谭嗣同故居

北半截胡同中的谭嗣同故居现已成为居民大杂院。

Former Residence of Tan Sitong

The former residence of Tan Sitong in Beibanjie Hutong has been converted into the house of common people.

南半截胡同中老宅门前的门墩
Gate piers in front of an old-style courtyard in Nanbanjie Hutong

清代国宾馆

　　这是位于南横东街 131 号的一座老院落，据传这里曾经是清代的国宾馆——会同馆，院落一角还存放着一口凤展翅荷花缸。

The State Guest House in Qing Dynasty

　　The No.131 courtyard in East Nangheng Street is an old-style courtyard , which is said to be the State Guest House in the Qing Dynasty. At the corner of the courtyard, there is a lotus vat decorated with the pattern of wing-spreading phoenix.

南横东街 是京城著名的古老街道,为城南第一东西方向的长街。街东头曾有建于明代的江南城隍庙、东岳天齐庙,西有三官庙、圆通观等。胡同中的全浙会馆为清代著名诗人龚自珍故居;109号为清两江总督曾国藩居所;民国初年邓颖超随母进京曾住在此街的湘阴会馆中,并在此院的平民义务学校初级班就读。

East Nanheng Street is a well-known ancient street in Beijing, and the longest east-west street in the south of Beijing city. There used to be Jiangnan Chenghuang (Town God in Southern China) Temple, Dongyue Tianqi (literally Eastern Sacred Mountain Equaling with Heaven) Temple built on the eastern section of the street, and Sanguan (Three Administrators) Taoist Temple and Yuantong (Understanding) Temple on its western section. Quanzhe Guild Hall on this street was once the former residence of Gong

俯瞰南横东街与新辟的菜市口大街交汇处
A bird's eye view of the juncture of East Nanheng Street and new-built Caishikou Street

Zizhen, a famous poet in Qing Dynasty. No.109 Courtyard was once the residence of Zeng Guofan when he was appointed the governor of Liangjiang (extent of jurisdiction roughly including today's Jiangsu, Anhui, Shanghai and Jiangxi). Deng Yingchao and her mother once lived in Xiangyin Guild Hall in this street when they came to Beijing in the early years of the Republic of China. Also, she studied in the elementary class in the compulsory school for common people in this yard.

南横东街与米市胡同、珠朝街交汇处
The juncture of East Nanheng Street, Mishi Hutong and Zhuchao Street

米市胡同 明代因米粮集市于此而称米市口（西侧胡同为菜市口），胡同两侧房屋整齐，多大宅门、名人故居及会馆，清顺治时期的礼部尚书、乾隆年间的大学士、嘉庆朝的御史、咸丰时期的工部尚书均居于此。

Mishi (Rice Market) Hutong The Hutong was named after a rice and grain market here during the Ming Dynasty. West to the Caishikou (Entrance to Vegetable Market), it was known as Mishikou (Entrance to Rice Market). Houses and courtyards along both sides of the hutong were arranged orderly, which used to be the mansions, former residences of famous people and guild halls. During Qing Dynasty, Emperor Shunzhi's minister of Board of Rites, Qianlong's grand secretary, Jiaqing's imperial censor and

现存会馆6处，南海会馆是康有为居处，安徽泾县会馆为五四时期著名刊物《每周评论》编辑部所在地，陈独秀、李大钊曾为该刊主办人。

Xianfeng's minister of Board of Works all once lived here. There still exist 6 guild halls in this hutong. Of them, the Nanhai Guild Hall was once the residence of Kang Youwei; the Guild Hall of Jingxian County in Anhui Province used to be the editorial department of the *Weekly Review*, a famed magazine during the May 4th Movement in 1919 and launched by Chen Duxiu and Li Dazhao.

米市胡同中一户人家把原来的大门堵上当作房间，又在旁边开了一个门。
One family in Mishi Hutong blocks up the original gate to make a room and opens another gate beside.

这是米市胡同北口的一个老棺材铺，房沿木板上的刻字"自置四川建昌荫陈金丝楠木…""…各省花板一概俱全"依稀可见。

This is an aged coffin store at the northern entrance to Mishi Hutong. Letterings of " Nanmu from Yin Chen, Jian Chang, Sichuan purchase by self" and " Here various colored board from every provinces" on the board are vaguely distinguishable.

康有为故居

康有为故居,在米市胡同南海会馆内,因院内有七棵树故名"七树堂"。康有为25岁时应顺天乡试初居此处,以后多次来京均住在这里。他曾在会馆的"汗漫舫"编书,1894年与梁启超等在此联合进京举子酝酿公车上书,使这里成为戊戌变法的活动中心。

Former Residence of Kang Youwei

The former residence of Kang Youwei is situated in Nanhai Guild Hall in Mishi Hutong. It is called "Seven Trees Hall", because there are seven trees in the yard. Kan Youwei lived here when he attended the Provincial Examination of Shuntian Prefecture at the age of 25 for the first time. Later, he resided here for many times when he came to Beijing. He once compiled books in " Han Man Fang " in the guild hall. In 1894, Kang Youwei and Liang Qichao collaborated with candidates for the imperial examinations to petition for the reform and the hall became the center of Reform Movement of 1898.

平坦胡同与中兵马街交汇处　The juncture of Pingtan Hutong and the Middle Bingma (Soldiers and Horses) Street

平坦胡同　在米市胡同东侧,原称扁担胡同。因其形状为两个大胡同中间夹有一条小胡同,相连一起呈"工"字形,故名。昔日,北京城内这种形状的街巷有20多个,均称扁担胡同,为避免混淆以谐音改为"平坦胡同"。旧时胡同东口有一观音庵,香火旺盛,胡同中均为民居。

Pingtan (Flat) **Hutong** is located to the east of Mishi Hutong and was called Biandan (Carrying Pole) Hutong in the past. The name came from the special layout of the hutong: a small lane is sandwiched by two larger ones at both ends, shaped like the Chinese character " 工". In the past, there were over 20 such hutongs of this layout in Beijing, and they were all named Biandan. In order to distinguish the identical pronunciation, the name of this alley was changed into " Pingtan Hutong". In old times, there was a Guanyin Nunnery located at the eastern entrance to this hutong, which enjoyed large numbers of worshipers. Now all the houses in this Hutong are resided by common people.

胡同中的一座旧宅门,门上写有对联:"名教自有乐地""诗书是我良田",门前只剩下孤零零的一只门墩。

An old-style gate in the hutong. There is a couplet on it, which reads: "Famed religions certainly find its own world, while Confucian classics served as my fertile land". Here now only a lonely gate pier is left.

北大吉巷 明朝时称打劫巷,清称打街巷,因名称不雅故谐音改为大吉巷。胡同中住有多位曲艺界及梨园界名人,如已故大鼓表演艺术家白云鹏曾住3号院;著名京剧演员时慧宝住7号院;22号院为李万春故居。

North Daji Lane was called Dajie (Robbing) Lane in the Ming Dynasty while Dajie (same pronunciation but meaning quarrel in the street) in Qing Dynasty. It sounds so offensive that the hutong was renamed Daji (Great Auspicious), roughly the same as its original name. There once lived many celebrities of folk art and Opera circles, such as Bai Yunpeng, the late artist of Beijing *dagu*, in No.3 Courtyard; Shi Huibao and Li Wanchun, both being celebrities of Beijing Opera, in No.7 and No.22 courtyards respectively.

北大吉巷一个沿街门脸和别具特色的云纹门墩
A store facing the street and unique gate piers with pattern of clouds in North Daji Lane.

北大吉巷一个四合院中的双层小楼
A small two-floor building in a Siheyuan in North Daji Lane

南大吉巷 原称羊肉胡同，1965年整顿街巷名称时，因京城有十余条羊肉胡同，此巷在原大吉巷之南故改称南大吉巷。胡同西端南侧为旌德会馆。南大吉巷虽然胡同狭窄，但干净整洁，交通方便，人民安居乐业。

South Daji Lane was once called Yangrou (Mutton) Hutong. There were some ten hutongs named Yangrou when the government uniformed the names of alleys and lanes in 1965. So it was changed to the current name, for it is located to the south of former Daji Lane. Jingde Guild Hall is situated on the south of the western section of the lane. Although it is narrow, the clean and neat lane offers convenient traffic and comfortable living environment to the local residents.

儒福里 清初称大猪营，清末的《京师坊巷志稿》称此地为东珠营。民国初期，通县电话局长王席儒在此建"如福里"。因王曾掩护董必武作革命工作，董老赠书"儒福里"刻于西端门洞之上。此胡同中有北京著名的"过街楼"，建于清朝道光年间，楼之北有砖刻"金绳"二字，楼之南侧为"觉岸"二字。（已消失，摄于 1994 年）

Rufuli Lane was called Dazhuying (Campsite of Big Pig) in early Qing. As stated in the *Jingshi Fangxiang Zhigao*, or *Records of Lane and Alley in Capital* of the late years of the dynasty, it was called Dongzhuying (Camp of Eastern Peals). During the early years of the Republic of China, Wang Xiru, the director of telephone bureau of Tongxian County built "Rufuli (literally, lane of happiness as wishes)". Vice Chairman Dong Biwu once granted his writing "Ru Fu Li (lane of Confucius and happiness)" to Mr. Wang and carved it on the gate in the west, for Wang once covered Dong to conduct revolutionary work. There was a famous building Guojielou (Cross Street Tower) in this lane, which was built in the reign of Qing Emperor Daoguang. The tablet inscribed with "Jin Sheng" is hung on the northern gate and another one " Jue An " on the southern gate. Now the tower is no longer exists (this photo taken in 1994).

小星胡同 位于报国寺西侧，原称小嘴巴或小醉芭胡同，1965年与大星胡同相对应改称小星胡同。古旧的街门上贴有民俗味极浓的门神和大红门联，绿树掩映着斑驳的院墙，古色古香，幽静安祥。活泼的儿童在胡同中玩起篮球，使古老的街巷充满了青春的活力。试看若干年后，将有多少体坛明星是曾闪耀在大星、小星胡同中的童星。（已拆除）

Xiaoxing (Little Star) **Hutong**　is located to the west of Baoguo (Serving the Country) Temple and was once called Xiaozuiba (literally, little mouth, or little drunken plantain) Hutong. Corresponding to Daxing (Big Star) Hutong, it was renamed as Xiaoxing Hutong in 1965. Gates facing the street are posted with door-gods and bright red couplets of strong folk customs. The green trees shroud the mottled walls. The tranquil alley is imbedded in the antique flavors. However, lively children are playing the basketball in the alley, which brightens the whole alley with youth energy. In the future, it is possible that many sports stars may come from those playing children. (It no longer exists.)

三庙街 位于宣武区北部,是一条远自唐代已成型的古老街道。明代因这里有一紫金寺而称紫金寺街。清代此街向东伸延,由于其东上斜街25号有"头庙",111号为"二庙",原街内还有一个庙,东西排列三座庙(均为关帝庙),清代《乾隆京城图》上已标为三庙街。此街虽古老破旧,但交通方便,故居民众多,喧阗热闹。

Sanmiao Street is located in the north of Xuanwu District. This aged street came into being as early as Tang Dynasty. It was called Zijinsi Street, for there stood a Zijin (Purple Golden) Temple in Ming Dynasty. During the Qing Dynasty, it extended eastward, with three temples (all were temples of Lord Guan) from the east to the west: one in No.25 in East Upper Slanting Street, one in No.111 Courtyard and the other in the original street. So it was marked as " Sanmiao (Three Temples) Street" on the *Map of Entire Beijing during Qianlong's reign*. This aged and shabby street has convenient traffic and large numbers of residences, bustling with activity.

三庙街、上斜街、下斜街及河沿三巷交汇处
The juncture of Sanmiao Street, Upper Slanting Street, Lower Slanting Street and the 3rd Lane of Heyan (Riverbank)

三庙街西街内老门前的葡萄架
Grape racks in front of an old gate on the West Sanmiao Street.

上斜街中有三忠祠，右图右侧
为现存的一座旧庙门。

The Sanzhong (Three Loyal
Officials) Memorial Temple in the
hutong. An ancient gate of a temple
still could be found to this day (right
in the right picture).

上斜街 明朝时称西斜街。因早年是河流故道，故西
高东低，路面较宽，但斜而不直。胡同中有三忠祠，为明代天启年
间(1624年)祭祀山西三位抗清官员的祠庙，清代改为山西会馆。
这里的广东会馆曾是清代诗人龚自珍和维新派领袖康有为的住
处；东莞新馆是清初年羹尧生活过的地方；河南会馆是民族英雄
林则徐的故居。

Upper Slanting Street was called the Western Slanting Street in
Ming Dynasty. This alley was formerly a watercourse. Sloping from west
to east, it is relatively wide, but not straight. There is a temple called
Sanzhong (Three Loyal Officials) in memory of the 3 loyalists of Shanxi
Province against the aggression of Manchu during the reign of Ming Em-
peror Tianqi (1624). It was converted into Shanxi Guild Hall in Qing
Dynasty. Guangdong Guild Hall also in this alley used to be the residences
of Gong Zizhen, a famous poet of Qing Dynasty and Kang Youwei, leader
of the Reform Movement of 1898. Dongguan New Guild Hall was the
former residence of Nian Gengyao, a famed general during Qing Emperor
Yongzheng's reign. Henan Guild Hall was the former residence of Lin
Zexu, a national hero.

原广东会馆旧址　Former site of Guangdong Guild Hall

上斜街的一座老院门，人们为了进出方便，把门槛去掉了。（已消失）

A gate of an old yard on the Upper Slanting Street. The threshold has been removed away for the convenience of passing.

下斜街　明代与上斜街相连，同称西斜街。清代改称槐树斜街，因街南口有土地庙又称土地庙斜街。《燕京岁时记》载：土地庙自正月起，凡初三，十三，二十三日有庙市。市无名物，唯花厂，鸽市差为可观。这条古老的胡同是元代连接北京新旧城的捷径。元大都建成后（1285 年）人们自新城到金中都旧城游览，就从这条自东北斜向西南的宽敞平坦的斜街上走过。胡同中有畿辅先哲祠，是清代洋务运动创始人张之洞的别墅。

Lower Slanting Street was linked up to the Upper Slanting Street in Ming Dynasty, and they were together called Western Slanting Street. It was renamed as Huaishu (Chinese Scholartree) Slanting Street in Qing Dynasty for a while, and then Tudimiao (Temple of God of Local Land) Slanting Street, for there was a land god temple at the southern entrance to the street. According to the *Yanjing Suishi Ji (Annual Customs and Festivals in Yanjing)*, starting from the first lunar month, temple fairs would be held in the 3rd, 13th and 23rd days of each month; there were no valuable articles on the fairs except the flourishing trade of flowers and pigeons. This ancient alley once served as the shortcut linking the new city and old city during the Yuan Dynasty. People used to walk along this northeast-southwest slanting street to make a tour in the old city of Zhongdu of Jin when the Dadu of Yuan was established in 1285. There was a Jifu Xianzhe (Sage in and around the Capital) Ancestral Temple on this street, which was once the villa of Zhang Zhidong, the founder of the Westernization Movement in Qing Dynasty.

校场口胡同 此为宣武门外大街路西的主干道之一，街面较宽，人来车往川流不息，两侧店铺鳞次栉比，是一条喧闹的街巷。据明代张爵著《京师五城坊巷胡同集》载："宣北坊有将军教场一二三四五条胡同。"清代朱一新著《京师坊巷志稿》中有"教场口，井一"的记载。

清朝定都北京以后，实行了旗、民分城居住的制度，内城以皇城为中心，由八旗分立四隅八方，各旗都在所驻门外设教场、演武厅，熟练骑射，操练技勇，校场口就是明、清两朝教场的出入路口。

Jiaochangkou (Entrance to Drill Ground) **Hutong** is one of the main lines to the west of Xuanwumenwai Street. People and cars flow in steady stream along the wide street, and numerous stores stand on both sides, making it a busy street. As stated in the *Jingshi Wucheng Fangxiang Hutong Ji (Collection of Hutongs of Five Districts in the Capital)* by Zhang Jue in Ming Dynasty, in Xuanbeifang there were a total of five hutongs named after Jiangjun Jiaochang (General's Drill Ground). And according to the *Jingshi*

Fangxiang Zhigao by Zhu Yixin in Qing Dynasty, there was a well at the entrance to the Jiaochang. When Qing moved the capital to Beijing, soldiers of Eight Banners and common people were ordered to reside in different sections. With royal city as the center, Inner City was stationed by the soldiers of Eight Banners. In order to practice horse riding and shooting, each banner set up its own drill ground. Jiaochangkou was the entrance to the drilling square both in Ming and Qing dynasties.

车子营北巷与校场口胡同交汇处　The juncture of North Cheziying (Carriage Camp) Lane and Jiaochangkou Hutong

校场三条　明代称将军教场三条胡同，清称将军教场三条，这是一条幽静的胡同，全长400米，宽4—6米，呈南北走向，北口路东2号为明代杨椒山祠（松筠庵）旁门。胡同中均为民居，充满了浓浓的京味。

Jiaochang Santiao was called Jiangjun Jiaochang Santiao (Third Lane of General's Drill Ground) Hutong in Ming Dynasty and Jiangjun Jiaochang Santiao Alley in Qing Dynasty. This tranquil alley, 400 meters long and 4-6 meters wide, goes from south to north. The No.2 Courtyard located at east of its northern section serves as side entrance to the Memorial Temple of Yang Jiaoshan (today's Songjun Hut), a Ming loyal official. All the houses in this alley are residences of common people with strong Beijing customs.

胡同中的居民生活悠闲自在
Easy life of the residents in the hutong

墙上的大"拆"字预示着这座四合院不久将被夷为平地　A huge Chinese character "拆" (demolishing) indicates that this Siheyuan will be removed soon.

海柏胡同 这是一条古老的胡同，明代称海波寺街，因有辽金时代的古刹海波寺而得名。清末民初改称海北寺街。1965年整顿街巷名称时改为海柏胡同。清朝著名文学家朱彝尊（号竹垞先生）曾在此处的顺德会馆居住。当年会馆中有藤花树两株、桠树一株，树旁太湖石垒砌成的自然台座，可坐而饮茶赋诗，其书房名为"古藤书屋"。竹垞先生在书屋中写成《日下旧闻》等北京重要地方文献。清代文学家孔尚任（著有《桃花扇》等）也曾在这个胡同中居住过。胡同中曾有广西颖州、沣州、潮州等会馆，今已全部拆除。

Haibai Hutong This ancient hutong was named Haibosi (Temple of Sea Waves) Street after the ancient temple with same name which was built in Liao and Jin dynasties. It was changed to be Haibeisi (Temple North to the Sea) Street during late years of Qing Dynasty and early years of the Republic of China. It was renamed as Haibai (Sea and Cypress) in 1965 when the government uniformed the names of alleys and lanes. Zhu Yizun (also named as Mr. Zhu Cha), a famous literati in Qing Dynasty, once lived in the Shunde Guild Hall in this hutong. Two vine trees and one Chinese tamarisk were planted here at that time, beside which was a natural desk piled with stones dug up from Taihu Lake. One can sit here drinking tea or composing poems. The study in the guild hall was called "Old Vine Study", in which Zhu Yizun finished *Rixia Jiuwen* (*Old Stories of the Capital*) and other literatures relating to the local history of Beijing. Kong Shangren (author of the *Taohuashan*, or *Peach Blossom Fan*), another prominent literati of Qing, also once lived in this hutong. Additionally, there used to be such guild halls as Yingzhou, Fengzhou and Chaozhou in this hutong, but they well all demolished.

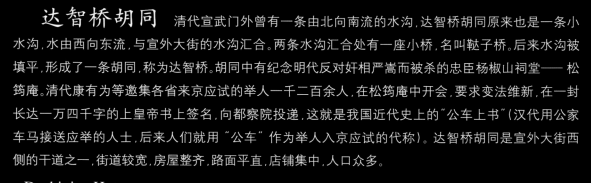

达智桥胡同

清代宣武门外曾有一条由北向南流的水沟，达智桥胡同原来也是一条小水沟，水由西向东流，与宣外大街的水沟汇合。两条水沟汇合处有一座小桥，名叫鞑子桥。后来水沟被填平，形成了一条胡同，称为达智桥。胡同中有纪念明代反对奸相严嵩而被杀的忠臣杨椒山祠堂——松筠庵。清代康有为等邀集各省来京应试的举人一千二百余人，在松筠庵中开会，要求变法维新，在一封长达一万四千字的上皇帝书上签名，向都察院投递，这就是我国近代史上的"公车上书"（汉代用公家车马接送应举的人士，后来人们就用"公车"作为举人入京应试的代称）。达智桥胡同是宣外大街西侧的干道之一，街道较宽，房屋整齐，路面平直，店铺集中，人口众多。

Dazhiqiao Hutong   There used to be a little stream running from north to south outside Xuanwu Gate in Qing Dynasty. The location of this hutong was also a stream running from west to east, which emptied into the stream aforesaid. There was a bridge over the crossing called Dazi (an offensive call for Tatar people in the old times) Bridge. Later, the stream was filled up and a hutong called Dazhiqiao (Achieving-Wisdom Bridge) emerged. In this hutong, there is a temple in memory of Yang Jiaoshan, a loyal minister who was killed due to his opposition against Yan Song, a treacherous Prime Minister in Ming Dynasty. Later the temple was renamed Songjun Hut. In late years of Qing Dynasty, Kang Youwei and other ardent reformers invited over 1,200 *Juren*s (the successful candidate in the imperial examinations at the provincial level in the Ming and Qing dynasties) to Songjun Hut. They signed their names on the 14,000-character petition to the Censorial Department calling for reforming. The event was historically known as the " Gongche Submitting Statement" (during the Han Dynasty, the Gongche, or government carriage, as a special honor was permitted to be used by those who attending the national examination, and then it referred in particular to *Juren* who came to the capital for the examination). The Dazhiqiao Hutong is one of arteries west to Xuanwumenwai Street. This wide, straight and populous street is lined with many stores and orderly residences.

胡同中杨椒山祠堂——松筠庵旧址
The former site of Songjun Hut (the Memorial Temple for Yang Jiaoshan) in this hutong.

达智桥胡同夜市灯火通明
Brightly lit night market in Dazhiqiao Hutong

五道街 在珠市口西大街西端北侧,是正阳、宣武二门之间"龙脉交通,车马辐辏之地",明代在此建五道庙以镇之,胡同因而称五道庙街。1965年整顿街巷名称时将五道庙头条、二条并入,统称五道街。此街汇合处可通樱桃斜街、铁树斜街、堂子街、韩家胡同和南新华街,交通方便、街景古朴,多老宅门。

Wudao (Five Roads) **Street** to the north of western section of West Zhushikou (Entrance to Pearl Market) Street is a traffic hub between Zhengyang Gate and Xuanwu Gate. During the Ming Dynasty, a temple named Wudao (it was supposed that there were five different roads for a person after death) was built to guard the area, so the hutong was named after it. In 1965 when the government uniformed the names of alleys and lanes, it, together with the first and the second lanes, was collectively re-named present name: Wudao Street. This street leads to Yingtao (Cherry) Slanting Street, Tieshu (Sago Cycas) Slanting Street, Tangzi (Hall) Street, Hanjia (Family Han) Hutong and South Xinhua (New China) Street, offering convenient traffic. It also features simple street scenes and numerous old courtyards and gates.

五道街上的一个老门脸,门板虽已破旧,但门额上的"鸿禧"两个大字依然苍劲有力。

An old and shabby gate in Wudao Street. The two Chinese characters " Hong Xi (Great and Happy)" on the gate remain bold and vigorous though the gate is old and shabby.

百顺胡同 明代此处种有柏树故名柏树胡同，清代取"百事顺遂"之意，更名为百顺胡同。这条胡同曾是中国京剧的发源地。京剧创始人程长庚曾住在胡同中的36号。程长庚生活在清代乾隆年间，是安徽潜山人，他率领徽剧戏班进京后将昆、弋诸腔融于皮、黄之中，被称为"徽班领袖"、"京剧鼻祖"。百顺胡同55号住过一位德高望重的京剧耆宿——陈德霖，他曾在程长庚的四箴堂科班学习青衣刀马旦，29岁选入清宫升平署，进宫演戏，深得慈禧太后赏识；50岁后被尊称为剧坊"老夫子"，为梅兰芳、尚小云等六大弟子传授技艺。胡同内曾有太平会馆。

Baishun Hutong Known as Baishu (Cypress) Hutong after cypress trees planted here during the Ming Dynasty, the hutong was renamed Baishun in the Qing, which means " Everything goes successfully as one wishes". The hutong served as the birthplace of Beijing Opera. Cheng Changgeng, one of the founders of Beijing Opera, once lived in No.36 Courtyard in this hutong. Cheng Changgeng, a native of Qianshan County in Anhui Province during Qing Emperor Qianlong's Reign, led his opera troupes came Beijing. They blended *kunqu*, *yiqiang* and other local operas with arias of Pi and Huang, forming a compete style and performing system that are shown today. Thus, he is praised as the " Leader of Hui Opera" and " Originator of Beijing Opera". Additionally, Chen Delin, a prominent and sainted actor of Beijing Opera, lived in No.55 Courtyard of this hutong. He studied the roles of *qingyi* and *daomadan* in Beijing Opera in Sizhentang (Four-Admonish Hall) a Beijing Opera school run by Cheng Changgeng. He was elected into Shengpingshu (Peaceful-Life Agency), an imperial troupe, at the age of 29 and was in Emperor Dowager's good graces. After 50 years old, he was honored as "Grand Old Man" in the opera troupe. He was also the teacher of Mei Lanfang, Shang Xiaoyun and other four students. There used to be Taiping Guild Hall in this hutong.

宣武区东南园胡同
Dongnanyuan (Southeastern Garden) Hutong in Xuanwu District

陕西巷 自明代迄今均为此称。清代此胡同中多会馆,著名的有济州会馆、四川东馆等。民国年间多妓院,营救蔡锷将军的小凤仙曾在此搭班,是较为繁华的商业街区,多旅馆、商店。与陕西巷相交的榆树巷是20世纪初京城名妓赛金花的宅第,现已是拥挤不堪的大杂院。

Shaanxi Alley The name of Shaanxi Alley dates back to the Ming Dynasty. There were many guild halls in this alley in Qing Dynasty, such as Jizhou Guild Hall and Eastern Hall of Sichuan. The alley was packed with brothels in the Republic of China. Xiao Fengxian, who rescued General Cai E, once lived here. There were a large number of inns and stores on this prosperous street. The Yushu (Elm) Lane crossing with Shaanxi Lane was once the residence of Sai Jinhua, a notorious prostitute in Beijing in the early years of the 20th century. It is a crowded yard now.

榆树巷与陕西巷交汇处 The juncture of Yushu and Shaanxi lanes

每当胡同里有崩爆米花的小贩到来时，都会吸引许多孩子前来观看。爆米花崩出时发出一声巨响，孩子们都捂起了耳朵。（图片为琉璃厂北柳巷，摄于1989年11月，现已拆除）

Many children would gather around the popcorn maker and cover their ears when the maker pops out the corn. (The lane does not exist, this photo was taken in North Willow Lane in Liulichang in November, 1989)

琉璃厂东、西街 是北京著名的图书文化街。辽金时期这一带称海王村,元朝时在海王村建起为宫廷烧制琉璃瓦的琉璃窑,明代修建北京宫殿,此处的琉璃窑被扩大为琉璃厂,直至清乾隆初期,地名就叫琉璃厂。1965 年以南新华街为界分为东、西琉璃厂街。

East and West Street of Liulichang (Glazed Tile Plant) is a well-known cultural street abundant in book stores in Beijing. It was called Haiwang (King of Sea) Village in Liao and Jin dynasties. Kilns manufacturing colored glazes for the royal palace were established here in Yuan Dynasty. The kilns were expanded into a plant when Ming Dynasty construted the palaces in Beijing. The name of Liulichang remained till the early years of the reign of Emperor Qianlong. The whole street was divided into two sections by South Xinhua Street as the boundary in 1965.

古朴典雅的东琉璃厂街景　Simple but elegant East Liulichang Street

琉璃厂图书文化街 最初形成于清乾隆年间,《琉璃厂书肆记》中记载这里有名盛堂、同升阁、二酉堂、文茂堂等。《宸垣识略》记春节厂甸情况:"厂前陈设杂技,锣鼓聒耳,游人杂遝,市肆玩好,书画、时果、耍具、无不毕集。"

Liulichang Cultural Street As a street full of book and antique stores, it took shape during the beginning of Qing Emperor Qianlong's reign. According to the *Liulichang Shusi Ji* (*Records of Bookstores on Liulichang Street*), there were many bookstores here including Mingshengtang, Tongshengge, Eryoutang and Wenmaotang. As stated in the *Chenyuan Shilue* (*Brief Introduction to Imperial City*), the Spring Festival at Changdian is as follows: Tourists swarmed around the acrobatics with gongs and drums sounding loudly. Various stalls selling books, paintings, vegetables, fruits and toys competed with each other.

东琉璃厂文化街上的文化商品琳琅满目 Various goods selling on the East Liulichang Cultural Street.

摆在橱窗里的木偶和皮影 Puppets and shadow-paly props behind the shop window

延寿街 在琉璃厂东部,原有一座规模宏大的寺庙名叫延寿寺,胡同因而得名。据《宸垣识略》记载:"延寿寺在辽、金时称巨刹,今之琉璃厂皆昔之寺基。北宋靖康元年(1126年)金兵攻陷宋都城,曾将宋徽宗、钦宗两个皇帝以及后妃等掳至中都城延寿寺内。元代寺庙已毁弃,明代仅存一块断碑,上书"大金延寿寺"。胡同南口西侧原有开业于清康熙八年(1669年)的王致和臭豆腐店,三百余年来,一直生意兴隆,声誉良好。李福寿制笔厂生产的毛笔也曾誉满京城。胡同中店铺、饭馆较多,是一条古老而繁华的街巷。

Yanshou Street is located to the east of Liulichang Street. There used to be a grand temple called Yanshou (Prolonging Life) Temple, and the street was named after the temple. As stated in the *Chenyuan Shilue*, it had been a grand temple in Liao and Jin dynasties and included the whole area of Liulichang. In 1126, the first year of under title of Jingkang, the troops of Jin Dynasty captured the capital of Northern Song Dynasty and took the two emperors, Huizong and Qinzong, and their consorts by force to this temple. The temple was damaged in Yuan Dynasty and till the Ming Dynasty there had left no trace except a broken stele inscribed with the Chinese characters "Great Yanshou Temple of the Jin Dynasty". A store of fermented bean curd called Wangzhihe was established on the west of this hutong at its southern entrance in 1669, or the 8th year of the Qing Emperor Kangxi's reign. It has had prosperous business and good reputation over these 300 years since its foundation. The writing brushes produced by Lifushou Brush Plant in the hutong are also well-known around Beijing. There are numerous stores and restaurants in this ancient and bustling hutong.

前青厂胡同　在琉璃厂街西侧,因当年琉璃窑烧窑取土,形成许多坑洼,积水成潭被称为"青厂潭",后改称青厂胡同。原有赴京赶考的举子暂住的四川、广西、汉中、榆林、顺德等会馆。

Front Qingchang Hutong is situated to the west of Liulichang Street. In the past time, the soil there was dug up to make colored glaze in the kilns, so many holes emerged and gathered the water, forming a pond called " Qingchang (Blue Plant) Pond". Later, the hutong was named after the pond. In the hutong, there were many guild halls such as Sichuan Guild Halls, Guangxi Guild Halls, Hanzhong Guild Hall, Yulin Guild Hall and Shunde Guild Hall, providing accommodations for the *Jurens* who attended the national examinations. These have already been converted into residences for common people.

铁树斜街一住户的门槛,由于长年踩踏,已成弯月形。

The threshold takes the form of a crescent due to the stamping of years in a household in Tieshu Slanting Street.

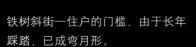

廊房二条　明朝称二条胡同,是由廊房头条派生出来的(位于头条南侧)。明清时为商业集中地,胡同中有二十来家玉器古玩铺,如三盛兴、恒盛兴、聚丰厚等,曾有"玉器大街"的称号。现胡同中店铺以经营服装为主,路北曾有瑞宾楼褡裢火烧铺,是著名的京味小吃,今已移至门框胡同中。

Langfang Ertiao (Second Hutong of Veranda House) was called Ertiao Hutong in Ming Dynasty, the name of which was derived from the Langfang Toutiao (First Hutong of Veranda House) located north to it. The hutong was the business hub in Ming and Qing dynasties. There are over 20 stores of jade and antiques, such as Sanshengxing, Hengshengxing, Jufenghou, and others, winning it a reputation " Jade Street". Today, most stores in this hutong are selling clothes. There used to be a shop on the north of the hutong called Ruibinlou selling *Dalian Huoshao* (baked wheaten cake in shape of *dalian*, a long, rectangular bag sewn up at both ends with an opening in the middle), which is a famous snack of Beijing flavor. Now, the store has moved to Menkuang (Doorframe) Hutong.

廊房三条　原为一条狭小的死胡同,因廊房头条派生而得名。胡同中曾为玉器作坊集中地,尚有几个银号,故有"银号街"之称。现为居民杂聚之处,沦为民居的临汾会馆尚依稀可见。

Langfang Santiao (Third Hutong of Veranda House) was a narrow blind hutong whose name derived from the Langfang Toutiao. In the past, many workshops processing jade articles grouped in the hutong, and it was also a concentrating place for *yinhao* (old-style Chinese private bank). So it was known as *Yinhao* Street. Today, residents are living here. Linfen Guild Hall which was converted into houses for common people is still vaguely obvious.

门框胡同 位于繁华的前门大街西侧，北起廊坊头条胡同，南至大栅栏街。清末，由当地商人集资在胡同中部建了一座过街财神佛楼，行人从南北方向看，过街楼下恰似一个门框，故而得名。这里自清代就是京城中有名的小吃街，曾经聚集着近二十家有名的小吃摊子，从南到北有复顺斋的酱牛肉，年糕王，豌豆黄宛，油酥火烧刘，馅饼陆，爆肚杨，厨子杨（年糕、炒饼、汤圆），年糕杨，豆腐脑白，爆肚冯，奶酪魏，康家老豆腐，炒火烧（把晾干的火烧横向切成薄片，与羊肉片一起炒），包子杨，同义馆涮羊肉，瑞宾楼（原名祥瑞）褡裢火烧，德兴斋的烧羊肉及白汤杂碎……由于味道鲜美，所以每天食客如云。

Menkuang (Doorframe) Hutong Located west to the flourishing Qianmen (Front Gate) Street, the Menkuang Hutong stretches from Langfang Toutiao in the north to the Dazhalan Street in the south. During the end of Qing Dynasty, local merchants raised fund and built Guojielou (Cross Street Tower) enshrining the God of Fortune in the middle of this hutong. Viewing from south to north, the tower resembled a doorframe, hence the name. The hutong has been renowned for snacks since the Qing Dynasty. More than 20 famous booths and stalls selling snacks of Beijing flavor grouped in this hutong, including pickled beef of Fushunzhai, Wang's glutinous rice cake, Wan's Pea-Flour Cake, Liu's crisp baked cake, Lu's mince pie, Yang's Quick-Fried Tripe, Chef Yang (selling glutinous rice cake, stir-fried cake and rice dumplings), Yang's Pea-Flour Cake, Bai's jellied bean curd, Feng's Quick-Fried Tripe, Wei's cheese, Kang's bean curd, stir-fried baked cake (stir-fried thin slice of dry backed cake with sliced mutton), Yang's steamed stuffed bun, instant-boiled mutton slices of Tongyiguan Restaurant, *dalian huoshao* of Ruibinlou (formerly named Xiangrui) Restaurant, cooked mutton and plain soup with sweetbread of Dexingzhai Restaurant, and so on. Eaters seeking for them came and converged there day after day only due to their various delicious tastes.

草厂十条胡同 元代大都城的城墙是由泥土堆积而成的。土城最怕雨淋水冲，因此每临夏秋之际都要"以苇蓑城"，就是用柴草当作遮雨的蓑衣，把土城掩盖起来。因此在各大城门附近都有贮存柴草的草厂，据统计明清之际全城尚有名为草厂的胡同三十余处。崇文门外两侧有以草厂为名的胡同十条，从西向东排列于西兴隆街南侧，这里老屋鳞次栉比且有会馆夹杂其中，多姿多彩的门楼、门墩，小巧精致的四合院，带有浓郁的城南民居风情，充溢着淳厚的京味儿和旧京民俗文化气息，因而1999年草厂三条至九条以及鲜鱼口街被列为北京市二十五片历史文化保护区之一。

Caochang Shitiao (Tenth Hutong) The city walls of Dadu of Yuan Dynasty was built of earth, so dry reed would be used to cover the wall in summer and autumn to prevent the city wall from being washed down by the rain. Therefore, Caochangs (warehouses for storing reed) were built around each of city gates. According to the statistics, there were more than 30 hutongs named as Caochang in Beijing during Ming and Qing dynasties, 10 of which were built beside Chongwen Gate. Standing to the south of Western Xinglong (Prospecting) Street from the east to the west, these hutongs are teemed with ancient houses and several guild halls among them. Gate-towers and gate piers of diverse styles and delicately laid out Siheyuans reveal a picture of strong flavor of Beijing life, as well as folk customs in south of the city. In 1999, from the third to ninth hutongs of Caochang, together with Xianyukou (Entrance to Fresh Fish) Street, were included on the list of 25 historical and cultural protection areas by Beijing municipal government.

草厂七条　Seventh Hutong of Caochang

草厂十条　Tenth Hutong of Caochang

草厂五条
Fifth Hutong of
Caochang

草厂横胡同
Horizontal Hutong of Caochang

崇文区西打磨厂胡同
West Damochang (Polishing Plant) Hutong in Chongwen District

整洁幽静的草厂三条
Tidy and serene Third Hutong of Caochang

西兴隆街 位于前门鲜鱼口街东部，明代为政府养羊和堆放草料之地，称为"羊坊草场"。清代这里有一座兴隆寺香火旺盛，故改称兴隆街。1965年将崇真观、东兴隆街并入，统称西兴隆街。

West Xinglong(Prospecting) **Street** is located to the east of Xianyukou (Entrance to Fresh Fish) Street in Qianmen Gate area. Here used to be the place called " Yangfang (Sheep Pasture) Caochang" where the government raised sheep and stacked the fodder in Ming Dynasty. The name of this street came from a Qing temple with the same name. The temple attracted a large number of pilgrims at the time. Chongzhenguan (Taoist Temple of Exalted Trueness) and East Xinglong Street were merged into this street in 1965 and the joint street was called West Xinglong Street.

西兴隆街北祥凤胡同
North Xiangfeng (Auspicious
Phoenix) Hutong to the north of
West Xinglong Street

崇文区薛家湾胡同　Xuejiawan (Family Xue's Bend) Hutong in Chongwen District

花市大街 在崇文门外，元朝时这里是大都城东南郊一个风光秀丽的游览胜地，有构筑别致的水木清华亭等园池。明朝永乐年间此地又成为存放神木的神木厂。清代以后改称花市大街，其周边有称为花市的小巷十余条纵横其间。

Huashi (Flower Market) Street is situated outside the Chongwen Gate. Located in the southeastern suburbs of the capital then, it was a charming scenic resort during the Yuan Dynasty. Uniquely designed gardens and pools including Shuimu Qinghua (literally, beautiful scene of water and plants) Pavilion were built there. The resort was converted into a warehouse in which divine timbers were stored during the reign of Ming Emperor Yongle. It has been called Huashi Street since Qing Dynasty. There are more than 10 hutongs named after Huashi running vertically and horizontally.

崇文区花市东三条（摄于 1988 年 3 月，已消失）
East Third Hutong of Huashi in Chongwen District

东便门城楼下的崇文区东花市铁辘轳把街的虎背口胡同（摄于 1988 年 3 月，已消失）
Hubeikou (Entrance to the Tiger's Back) on the Tieluluba (Iron Hold of Windlass) Street at the foot of Dongbian Gate Tower in Huashi, Chongwen District (photo taken in March, 1988)

俯瞰今日崇文门、东便门，可清晰看见惟一一段保留下来的北京内城城墙遗址

Overlooking today's Chongwen Gate and Dongbian Gate, one would find the only preserved section of the Inner City wall in Beijing

东西富贵

东城、西城是北京城的中心地带,它辖盖了原北京城的内城地区及城区边缘地带,是北京最具代表性、最具人文景观的地区。

元代,以三海水域为中心兴建大都城,紧傍什刹海东岸为纵贯全城的中轴线位置,以什刹海东西两岸的距离作为全城宽度的半数,修建了四面城墙。城内共设43坊(相当于今日街道办事处),东城区内就有保大、明照、澄清等16坊,西城区则有阜财、金城、集庆等19坊。大都城中街道非常整齐,由南北和东西走向的胡同构成规则的棋盘型。请看《马可·波罗游记》中描绘的大都胡同:

从什刹海看钟鼓楼
Viewing the Bell and Drum Towers from Shichahai

"全城的设计都用直线规划。大体上,所有街道全是笔直走向,直达城墙根。一个人若登城站到城门上,朝正前方远望,便可看见对面城墙的城门。城内的公共街道两侧,有各种各样的商店和货摊……新都的中央,耸立着一座高楼,上面悬着一口大钟,每夜鸣钟报时。第三次钟响后,任何人不得在街上行走。"

钟鼓楼是当时最繁华的商业中心,这里设有米市、面市、缎子市、帽子市、鸭鹅市、珠子市、铁市等。东四牌楼、西四牌楼也是买卖兴隆之处,东西两庙隆福寺和护国寺是东西两城著名的庙市,也是人文文化的集中体现处。

明、清两朝对元大都实行了缩北拓南的措施,并在元大都南墙遗址上修建起东西向的长街(今之东西长安街),明嘉靖年间修筑了简朴实用

的北京外城城墙。

明代的政治中心在东城一带,这里有规模浩大、气势恢宏的紫禁城,中央政权机构则集中在皇宫正门承天门(天安门)的南侧。其中户部、吏部、礼部、兵部、工部、钦天监、宗人府、太医院列于宫廷广场的东部,这些部门主要掌管休养生息事宜,包括官吏任命、赋税、户口等,故有"东边掌生"之说。而刑部、五军都督府、锦衣卫等掌握着全国杀伐大权及刑狱衙门则设在广场的西部,因而又有"西边掌死"之说。

清代的《天咫偶闻》一书载:"京师有谚云:东富西贵,盖贵人多住西城,而仓库皆在东城。"这是指当时东城朝阳门、东直门内外粮仓众多,有的已成为了胡同名称,如海运仓、北新仓、新太仓等,一些富商大贾及殷实人家多居于此,表面显得很富有;而西城的什刹海周围,西四以及西单迤北有许多王府,住着清朝的显贵,因而俗传"西贵"。但是到了民国初年,情况又有了变化,当时军阀混战,政局不稳,真个是"乱哄哄你方唱罢我登场",那些夺得实权的达官显贵大部分选择在日渐繁华的东城居住,尤其是朝阳门里、东四、王府井、景山东部,陆续出现了许多东西合璧的建筑,既标新立异又富丽堂皇,加之门卫森严,一时变得十分显赫,而一些商人则西移至西四、西单西南部,使丰盛胡同、辟才胡同、宣武门内大街一带显出了"富相",变成了"东贵西富"。这些"史迹",从王文波先生摄下的胡同照片中也可以见到一些蛛丝马迹。东城的一些大宅门作为胡同的细胞,从中更能观测出其富丽堂皇的本质和"旧时王谢堂前燕,飞入寻常百姓家"的变化。身处京城,无论是居住在"绿槐阴里,深深庭院",还是登高远眺"城门矗立,甲第连云"的广衢街巷,都是令人神往的。

The Wealthy and the Noble of Dongcheng and Xicheng Districts

Dongcheng (East City) and Xicheng (West City) districts, consisting of the inner and marginal areas of Beijing, are the central parts of the city. They boast of most typical human landscape in Beijing.

In Yuan Dynasty, the capital city was constructed with Sanhai (literally Three Seas, sea meaning small inland body of fresh water at the time) as the heart. The eastern bank of Shichahai (Ten-Temple Sea) Lake was selected as the central axis passing through the whole city. The all-round city walls were constructed with the distance between the eastern and western banks of Shichahai as the half of the width of the whole city. 43 fangs, whose function is equal of today's sub-district office, were established in the city. There were 16 fangs such as Baoda, Mingzhao and Chengqing in Dongcheng District and 19 fangs including Fucai, Jincheng and Jiqing in Xicheng District. The streets in the Dadu city were in striking order. The north-south hutongs and east-west hutongs intersect each other, forming a shape of chessboard. Marco Polo described hutongs in Dadu in his travel book, *The Travels of Marco Polo*, a book fascinated Europe at that time as follows:

" The whole city is designed in line with the straight lines. All streets go straight till the bottom of the city wall. Standing on a city gate, one could see the opposite city straightly. There are various stores and booths on both sides of the public streets... Positioned in the center of the new-constructed capital is a high tower, in which a giant bell was hung. The bell is beaten in the evening to mark time. No one would be allowed in the streets after its third strike."

The Bell and Drum Towers was the most prosperous business center at that time. There were rice market, flour market, satin market, hat market, duck and goose market, pearl market and iron article market. The businesses also boomed in Dongsi Pailou (decorated archway) and Xisi Pailou. As the sites of prominent temple fairs, the Longfu (Prosperity and Blessing) Temple in the east and Huguo (Defending the Country) Temple in the west were both the hubs of the cultures.

Both in Ming and Qing dynasties, the governments restrained the development in the north city and expanded the growth of the south city. A long avenue (today's Eastern Chang'an Boulevard and Western Chang'an Boulevard) was constructed on the relics of the southern city wall of Dadu in Yuan Dynasty. The simple and practical city walls of the Outer City of Beijing were built during Ming Emperor Jiajing's reign.

The eastern part of Beijing was the political center in Ming Dynasty. Here stood the large-scale and stately Forbidden City. The central authorities were located in the southern section of the front gate of imperial palace — Chengtian Gate (literally, the Gate of Heavenly Succession, today's Tian'an Gate, or Gate of Heavenly Peace). Among them, Board of Revenue, Board of Civil Official, Board of Rites, Board of War, Board of Works, Astronomical Bureau, Court of the Imperial Clan and Imperial Academy of Medicine were all set up to the east of square in the imperial palaces. These departments took charge of the issues such as nomination of officials, tax collection, registered permanent residence, etc. therefore, people used to say that the eastern part of the palace square controlled the life of people. In contrast, some departments like Board of Punishment, Five Chief Military Commissions and Jinyiwei (literally, Brocade Guards, a kind of state secret police) were situated to the west of the square. These authorities were empowered to execute death sentence and administrated the prisons. Similarly, people used to say that the western part of the palace square took the life of people.

As stated in *the Tianzhi Ouwen* (*Anecdotes Heard close to Heaven*), a famous sketchbook of Qing Dynasty, "There is a saying in the capital: the eastern area of the city was wealthy while the western area was noble, because the wealthy always lived in the eastern area, while storehouses were concentrated in the eastern area." At the time, huge amounts of barns were built around Chaoyang Gate and Dongzhi Gate, and many wealthy businessmen and families lived there, making the area looked affluent. Even today, many hutong's names are still used to mark the spots, such as the Haiyuncang (Sea-Transportation Granary), Beixincang (North New Granary), Xintaicang (New Rice Granary), and so on. In contrast, there were many princes' mansions in which many nobles lived around the Shichahai and the area west to Xisi and Xidan. Accordingly, common people used to say that the western part of Beijing was noble. However, situations changed at the beginning of the Republic of China. The warlords fought with each other and the whole country was plunged into chaos. The state power was transferred from one party to another. Those high-ranking officials seizing the real power chose to live in the booming eastern part of Beijing, especially the areas inside Chaoyang Gate, Dongsi, Wangfujing and east to Jingshan Park. Many novel and magnificent structures were built in the combined style of western and eastern cultures, and these brilliant buildings were guarded heavily, together forming a land of eminence. Then some merchants moved westward to Xisi and the southwestern part of Xidan. As a result, "wealthy looking" appeared around Fengsheng (Rich) Hutong, Picai (Firewood) Hutong and Xuanwumennei Street. The "noble eastern part and wealthy western part" came into being. We may found some historical traces from the pictures of Hutongs taken by Mr. Wang Wenbo. As the basic fabric of Hutong, some gates of past noble families may reflect the disappeared splendor and the constant state of flux of human life. The experiences of living in "isolated yards surrounded by ancient trees" or watching the streets encircled by "city walls standing tall and swarm of nobles' mansions" are really enchanting.

方家胡同 在雍和宫大街西侧,自明代至今均沿此称（文革中一度改为红日北路七条，很快恢复原名）。这是一条古老而幽静的胡同,这里有清代的循郡王府以及标准的四合院;也有民国初年高官显贵的大宅门;还有清朝末年开办的北京第一代图书馆——京师第一图书馆;驻有清朝神机营所属的内火器营马队厂和古老的寺庙——白衣庵等。

Fangjia (Family Fan) **Hutong** is located to the west of Yonghegong (Palace of Harmony and Peace) Lamasery Street and its name has been remained the same since Ming Dynasty (it was changed to be the Seventh Hutong of North Red-Flag Street during the Culture Revolution but regained the original name shortly). Standing in ancient and tranquil hutong, are not only Mansion of Prince Xun of the Qing Dynasty and typical siheyuan, but also splendor house-doors of those noble or wealthy families during the early years of the Republic of China. Additionally, there were the First Capital Library established during the end of Qing, battle-steed depot subordinate to the Inner Firearm Battalion of Divine Skill Division, as well as an old temple, Baiyi (White Clothes) Nunnery.

雨中的方家胡同疑似江南水乡
Fangjia Hutong in the rain features the quaint charms of water-towns found in the south of China.

循郡王府 据《啸亭续录》载：循郡王府在方家胡同。循郡王名永璋，是清乾隆皇帝的第三子。乾隆五十二年（1787年）按贝勒的等级修建循郡王府。此府分为东西两个院落，均坐北朝南。西院（现15号）正门临街，面阔3间，街南侧有照壁一座，门内原有正堂5间，东西配房各3间。东跨院原规模较大（现13号），属于花园和生活区。它又分主院、中院和后院，临街为倒座房，大门位于院落偏东。循郡王府庭院宽阔敞亮，房屋建筑整齐，但没有清代传统皇族府第形制。据传清末名妓赛金花曾在此居住过，后为伪华北政务委员会委员长王揖唐的住宅。

Mansion of Prince Xun According to the *Xiaoting Xulu* (*Continuation to the Miscellanea at Xiaoting Pavilion*), the mansion of Prince Xun was located in Fangjia Hutong. The prince, personal name Yongzhang, was the third son of Qing Emperor Qianlong. In 1787, the 52nd year of Qianlong's reign, the mansion was constructed in line with the standard of *beile* (third-grade prince), and comprised the eastern courtyard and western courtyard, both facing south. The front gate of the western courtyard (today's No.15 in the hutong), 3-bayed in width, faces a screen wall across the street. In the courtyard there used to be 5 principal rooms, as well as 3 subordinate rooms on both sides. The eastern courtyard (today's No.13 in the hutong), larger in scale, functioned as the living quarters with a garden. This courtyard is subdivided into three parts: principle yard, middle yard and rear yard. The Daozuofang (rooms with the doors facing the inner courtyard) backs onto the street while front gate was built in the east of the courtyard.

院内的一座月亮门
A moon gate in the courtyard

With a light and spacious courtyard, the Mansion of Prince Xun was orderly laid out, and all structures were designed in carefully planned order. However, one cannot find the ranking traces of Qing Dynasty here. It was said that Sai Jinhua, a notorious prostitute in the end of Qing Dynasty, once lived here. Later, Wang Yitang, the chairman of the North China Administrative Committee under the protection of the Japanese government, resided here. At present, it is the dormitory building of the Ministry of Foreign Affairs and Recreational Center of Old Officials in Dongcheng District. The No.15 yard in this hutong is owned by a school-run factory at present.

庭院内青砖墁地，宽阔整洁
The roomy and trim courtyard covered by black and blue bricks

前永康胡同 位于雍和宫南侧,因明朝时永康侯徐忠的住宅在此而得名。清宣统时,因胡同中有一明代所建的观音寺而更名观音寺,1965年整顿街巷名称时将观音寺与前永康胡同合并,改称前永康胡同。今7号、9号四合院相传为清末太监李莲英所建,门前八字影壁十分引人。1949年后,徐海东、陈毅曾先后在此居住过。

Front Yongkang (Eternal Health) **Hutong** is located to the south of Yonghegong Lamasery and its name originated from the house of Marquis Yongkang Xu Zhong in Ming Dynasty. During the Qing Emperor Xuantong's reign, it was renamed Guanyin (Avalokitesvara) Temple Hutong due to a Ming temple with the same name in this hutong. In 1965, the hutong got its present name by merging Guanyin Temple Hutong and Front Yongkang Hutong. The No.7 and No.9 yards were said to be built by Li Lianying, a eunuch in the end of Qing Dynasty. The screen wall like the Chinese character " 八 " in front the of gate is especially appealing. After 1949, the General of the PLA Army Xu Haidong, Marshall Chen Yi once lived here successively.

影壁上的砖雕图案精美、细腻
The delicate and exquisite designs carved on the bricks of the screen wall.

八字大影壁
The great screen wall

国子监街 旧称成贤街，因为孔庙和国子监在街内符合"左庙右学"的规制，而且街头立有四座过街牌坊，东西街口牌坊题额为"成贤街"。这是京城中具有近七百年历史的老街巷。胡同中那亭亭如盖的老槐树，映衬着巍然耸立的过街牌楼和古老的房屋，呈现出了古都北京古文化街的独特风貌。

　　国子监是我国古代的最高学府，也是掌管国学政令的机关。元代称太学，明永乐时改称国子学，清代称国子监。元、明、清三代在此培养了大批人才，其中包括俄国、缅甸、朝鲜、越南等国的留学生。这里既是古代中华人才荟萃之地，也是中外文化交流的场所之一。

Guozijian Street It was once called Chengxian (Achieving the Virtue) Street. Guozijian (Imperial College) on the street is located immediately to the west of the Temple of Confucius, a typical layout according to the Chinese ancient architectural rule, which indicates that the institution should be built on the right while the Temple of Confucius built on the left. A total of 4 memorial archways were erected over the street. Among them, the archways stand at the eastern and western entrances to the street bear the inscriptions of the street name. This ancient alley enjoys a history of nearly 700 years. The imposing archways, antique houses and prosperous pagoda trees standing towering with canopy of leaves together display unique features of this ancient street of culture.

As the highest educational institution in ancient China, the Guozijian administered the national education and political orders. It was called Taixue during Yuan Dynasty and renamed as Guozixue during Emperor Yongle's reign in Ming Dynasty. It gained its current name Guozijian in Qing Dynasty. Legions of talented people were educated here during Yuan, Ming and Qing dynasties, including many foreign students from Russia, Burma, Korea and Viet Nam and etc. It was once not only gathering place of Chinese ancient talents, but also a venue for cultural exchange between China and foreign countries.

国子监大门
Front Gate of Guozijian

成贤街牌坊
Memorial Archway on Chengxian Street

官书院胡同　位于孔庙东墙外，东边隔墙与雍和宫相望，是一条南北方向的小胡同。清末称小后井，民国二十六年(1937年)改称官书院。胡同中有一幅门联曾广为流传，上联是：东边胤禛去往皇城当帝王；下联是：西侧孔丘来到京师为圣人；横批为：以邻为荣。它如实地反映了这条京城小巷的"左有帝王、右有圣人"的特殊位置。

Guanshuyuan Hutong is located outside the eastern wall of the Temple of Confucius, separated from the Yonghegong Lamasery by a wall in the east. This south-north small hutong was known as Xiaohoujing (Little Rear Well) during the end of Qing Dynasty, and in 1937, the 26th year of Republic of China, it got present name: Guanshuyuan (Courtyard of Official Books). A pair of couplets hanging in this hutong had acquired a proverbial currency, which reads: in the east Yinzhen (Emperor Yongzheng) goes to the Royal City to be the emperor; while in the west Kong Qiu (Confucius) comes to the capital to be a sage. The horizontal scroll bears an inscrip-

老舍故居 在东城区灯市口西街北侧的丰富胡同 19 号。小小的黑色院门坐西朝东,院门内有一座贴着大红福字的影壁,充满了浓郁的京味。正对院门是一个庭院和两间南房,两侧是一狭长小院,北边为一座三合院,院内东西各有三间厢房,北房三间,两边各带一间耳房。明间和西次间是客厅,东次间为卧室。西耳房是老舍先生的书房,著名话剧《方珍珠》《龙须沟》《茶馆》等均在此写出。

院中花木扶疏,正房前有两棵柿子树,为老舍先生亲手所植。金秋时节,红色柿子缀满枝头,院子被称为"丹柿小院",据说这是老舍先生于1950年用100匹白布"换"来的。

Former Residence of Lao She is located in No.19 of Fengfu (Abundance) Hutong which is situated on the north of West Dengshikou (Entrance to Market of Lantern) Street in Dongcheng District. The small black gate facing the east and the screen wall pasted with a huge red " Fu (happiness)" imbue the whole yard with strong flavor of Beijing style. Inside the front gate, a sub-yard with two rooms facing north is flanked with a narrow courtyard on each side. To its north is a three-walled sanheyuan, in which there are 3 wing-rooms, 3 principal rooms with a house attached on each side. The main house and western secondary house used to be the drawing rooms and the eastern secondary house was the bedroom. The side room in the west was the study of Mr. Lao She. It was in this study that Lao She created many famous play scripts and novels, including *Pearl Buck*, *Longxu (Dragon-Beard Ditch) Slum*, *Teahouse*, and others. Among the luxurious flowers and trees in the courtyard, two persimmon trees planted by Lao She himself stands in front of the main house. During the autumn, these two trees are full of persimmons. Accordingly, the yard is called " Red Persimmon Yard". As the story goes, this yard was " bartered" by Lao She with 100 bolts of cloth.

带假山石的庭园显示着主人身份的显赫　The court with artificial hills demonstrates the eminent status of the owner.

院中的垂花门保存完好
Well-preserved tassel gates in the courtyard

帽儿胡同　在地安门外大街东侧，明代因有道教寺庙文昌宫而称为梓潼庙文昌宫，清代改称帽儿胡同。今胡同 21 号即为文昌宫旧址，原有山门、前殿、中殿及后配殿等，现为帽儿胡同小学。今 9 号、11 号为清朝官员的私人宅园，名为"可园"（为清朝大学士文煜所建），住宅部分共有五进院落，院内有照壁、影壁、屏门。在一座雕刻精美的垂花门两侧，有一对造型生动的小石狮。胡同中的 35 号、37 号为宣统皇后婉容的娘家，俗称娘娘府。45 号为清提督衙门（俗称北衙门），北洋军阀冯国璋曾在此居住。

Maoer Hutong, located to the east of Di'anmenwai Street, was once called Zitongmiao Wenchanggong (Palace of Literal Prospect) during the Ming Dynasty, for there was a Taoist temple so named in the hutong. It was changed to Maoer (Cap) Hutong in Qing Dynasty. A primary school having the same name was built on the site of the Wenchanggong, the No. 21 courtyard, in which there used to be the front gate, front hall, middle hall, secondary hall in the back and other structures. The No.9 and No.11 courtyards were once private residences owned by Qing officials, known as Keyuan Garden. It was believed that Wen Yu, a high-ranking official of Qing Dynasty, built the garden. The whole residence consists of 5 courtyards, built with screen wall, shadow wall and screen gate. There is a pair of vivid stone lions flanking the exquisitely carved tassel gate. The No.35 and No.37 courtyards were the parent's home of Wanrong, empress of the last emperor of China, Xuantong. So, they were once commonly called Niangniang's Mansion. The No.45 Courtyard was once the office building of provincial commander-in-chief in the Qing Dynasty (commonly called Beiyamen, or North *Yamen*). The Northern Warlords Feng Guozhang once lived here.

79

帽儿胡同 37 号院大门。门上的油漆已经脱落，露出了木板。一对铜制门钹也已经变成了青绿色，只有右边的一个经常被敲门人触摸，保持着黄铜的金黄色。这里是清朝宣统皇后婉容的娘家，她就是从这个大门走出嫁入皇宫，成为中国末代皇帝溥仪的皇后。

A front gate of No.37 Courtyard in Maoer Hutong. The paint has come off and the wooden board appears. The bronze cymbal-shaped articles on gates have turned into green, but the right knocker keeps the golden color of the brass due to the frequent touch by visitors. The courtyard was parents' home of Wanrong. It was through this gate that she made her farewell to her parents and walked into the imperial palace, becoming the empress of Puyi, the last emperor of China.

拐杖胡同　在地安门外大街东侧，因其形状似一根拐杖而得名。全长200余米，清朝属于镶黄旗，胡同中多为古旧民居。

Guaibang (Crutch) Hutong is located to the east of Di'anmenwai Street. The name came from its shape that is extremely similar to a crutch. The alley is over 200 meters long. It belonged to the Xianghuangqi (Bordered Yellow Banner) in Qing Dynasty, one of the royal Eight Banners. Most residences in the hutong have a long history.

一扇老门和两个门墩
An aged gate and a pair of gate piers

东城区福祥胡同　Fuxiang (Happy and Auspicious) Hutong in Dongcheng District

东不压桥胡同 在地安门外大街东侧，明代称布粮桥，这是元代通惠河经皇城主河入什刹海的干流上的主要桥梁，再向北就是著名的后门桥（万宁桥）。当年布粮桥畔是交易布匹、粮食的集市，胡同因桥而得名。另有一种说法是与北海后门西压桥相对而言的。北海后门外原有皇城北墙，这道城墙从桥上而过，也就是"压"在桥上，所以称西压桥。而东边的皇城墙与布粮桥有一段距离，为与西压桥相对称，故名东不压桥，老北京有一句俗话："西压东不压"指的就是这两座位于皇城北侧的桥梁。

Dongbuyaqiao (Eastern Non-Pressed Bridge) Hutong is located to the east of Di'anmenwai Street. There was a bridge named Buliang (Clothes and Grain) during the Ming Dynasty. This bridge was the main bridge in Dadu of the Yuan Dynasty where Tonghui River emptied into the Shichahai Lake. Around the bridge there used to be a market for Clothes and Grain, hence the bridge name. Then the hutong was named after the bridge, which gradually became Dongbuya by mispronunciation. To the further north is famous Houmen (Rear Door, i.e. Wanning, or Eternal Peace) Bridge. Another story goes that the name corresponds to the Xiya (Western Pressed) Bridge at the back gate of Beihai Park. The former northern walls of royal city strode over a bridge, namely it "pressed" on the bridge. Hence, the bridge was called "Pressed Bridge in the west", or Western Pressed Bridge. In contrast, there was certain distance between the eastern walls of royal city and Buliang Bridge. In order to correspond to the " Pressed Bridge in the west", it is called " Non-pressed Bridge in the east", or Eastern Non-Pressed Bridge. There was a folk saying in old Beijing that Pressed in the west and non-pressed in the east, which indicated the two bridges to the north of the royal city.

过春节了，交道口北二条中的一个住户把自己的家装点得格外漂亮。
A decorated house more brilliantly than usual in Beiertiao (Northern Second Hutong) of Jiaodaokou (Entrance to Crossing Roads) Street in the Spring Festival.

（后页）从高处俯视北京胡同和四合院，于斑驳杂乱中透出古朴之气。
(Next page) A bird's eye view of Hutongs and Siheyuans in Beijing, emanating an atmosphere of primitive simplicity in the mess.

四合院大门上的精美砖雕
Exquisitely carved bricks over the
front gate of Siheyuan

秦老胡同中一座被保护的四合院修葺一新，重显昔日风采。
A well-preserved Siheyuan that has been reconstructed redisplays
the past brilliance in Qinlao (Old Man Qin) Hutong.

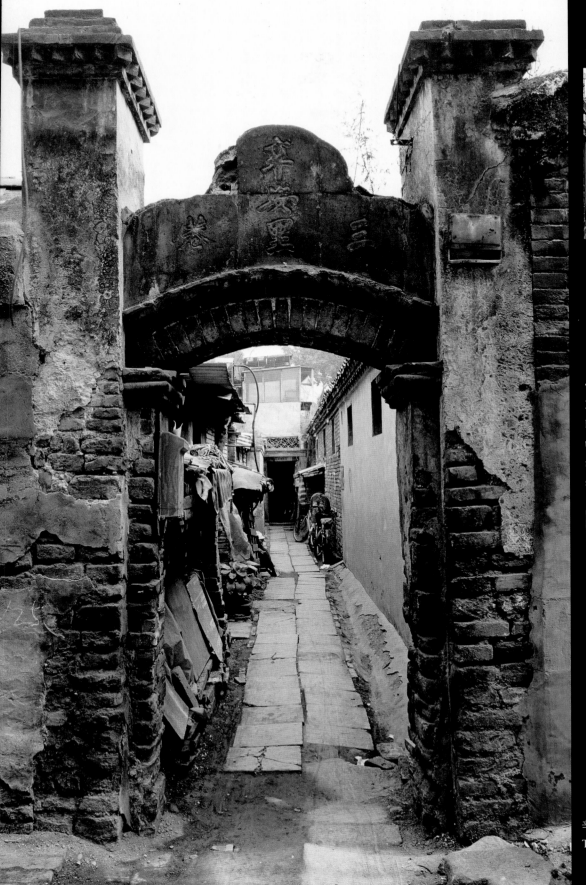

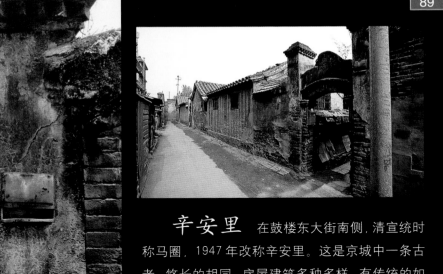

辛安里 在鼓楼东大街南侧，清宣统时称马圈，1947年改称辛安里。这是京城中一条古老、悠长的胡同，房屋建筑多种多样，有传统的如意门，也有东西合璧的拱形门。

Xin'anli Lane, to the south of East Gulou Street, was called "horse stall" during the reign of Qing Emperor Xuantong. In 1947, it was renamed as Xin'anli. This ancient long hutong boasts of buildings of various styles, including traditional Ruyi (an S-shaped ornamental object, usually, made of jade, formerly a symbol of good luck) gate and arch-shaped gate with oriental and western styles.

辛安里四巷的门楼
The gate tower in the Fourth Hutong of Xin'anli

辛安里三巷
The Third Hutong of Xin'anli

王 大 人 胡 同　现称北新桥三条，据传明代太监王承恩的宅第曾在此，清代改为理郡王府，民国时王府荒废，王府西侧的广恩寺曾为国民党要员何应钦的别墅。

Wangdaren (Dear Mr. Wang) Hutong, now called the Beixinqiao Santiao (Third Hutong of North New Bridge), is said to be the mansion of Wang cheng'en, a eunuch of Ming Dynasty. It was converted to be the Mansion of Prince Li in Qing but had fallen into disuse during the Republic of China. Guang'en (Extensive Favor) Temple, to the west of this prince mansion, was once the villa of He Yingqin, an important high-ranking official of Kuomintang (KMT).

小院有喜事
（1983 年 10 月摄于王大人胡同）

Happiness in the little yard
(Taken in Wangdaren Hutong in October 1983)

20世纪八九十年代，京城兴起做家具的热潮，许多北京人纷纷自购木料和板材，请木工来家里做家具（1990年5月摄于鼓楼东大街）

During the 1980's, self-made furniture grew into fashion. Many Beijingers purchased timbers and boards, and hired woodworkers to make furniture (taken in East Gulou Street in May 1990).

（1981年6月摄于崇文门北大街）
North Chongwenmen Street
(taken in June 1981)

节日的南锣鼓巷，居民们张贴对联和福字，把灯笼挂在大门外。
Nanluogu (South Gong and Drum) Lane in the Spring Festival. Residents posted couplets and "Fu" (happiness) character and hung the lanterns outside the gate.

东棉花胡同

明朝时，此地为棉花市场，从明迄清均称棉花胡同。胡同东头路北有一大宅院，精雕细刻的砖雕门楼引人注目。据说此宅为清末一位刘姓将军的住宅，宅为三进院落，最具特色的是二门的砖雕。二门高4米多，宽约2.5米，为拱券型，从金刚墙以上刻有花卉、走兽，顶部为朝天栏杆，栏板上刻有岁寒三友，门两侧雕有多宝阁，阁内有暗八仙图案。

Dongmianhua (East Cotton) **Hutong** The hutong was named after a cotton market during the Ming Dynasty, and the name has not been changed. Standing north at its east end is a large mansion, whose eye-catching gate tower was built with delicately carved bricks. It was said this mansion was once the residence of a general surnamed Liu in the Qing Dynasty. The whole courtyard is divided into 3 sections. The most attracting feature is the carved bricks on the second gate. This arch-shaped gate is more than 4 meters high and around 2.5 meters wide. Flowers and animals are engraved above the Jingang (diamond) wall. The gate is topped with stone pillars and balustrade richly decorated with Chinese traditional pattern of Suihan Sanyou (three cold-resistant friends of winter, i.e. pine, bamboo and plum). Treasure cabinets are carved on both sides of the gate, with the design of Eight Immortals.

旧鼓楼大街 在钟鼓楼西侧。元代此处建有齐政楼，明代时塌毁，后来在齐政楼东部重建鼓楼，又在其北建钟楼。钟鼓楼是历代帝王之都的标志性建筑，始终与都城皇宫相伴相存，是元、明、清三朝报时的场所，古韵悠长，历史久远。

齐政楼又称旧鼓楼，是针对明代所建鼓楼而称。旧鼓楼大街亦沿此称。这是一条古老的街道，原来北端仅到城墙之下，往北不能通行。北端西侧有药王庙，香火旺盛，故清代此街曾称药王庙街。现庙已废，仅存广济寺（双寺之一）。旧鼓楼大街南端多老店铺、老民居，且有粗大的百年古槐。

老店铺门脸的痕迹依稀可见（已拆除）
Dim traces of gates of aged stores and shops
(it no longer exists because of the expansion of the street).

Jiugulou (Former Drum Tower) **Street** was to the west of the Bell and Drum Towers. There stood Qizheng (Orderly Administration) Tower in Yuan Dynasty. Being destroyed during Ming Dynasty, it was reconstructed later on the present site, east to its original position. Shortly, a bell tower was built to its north. As the symbol structures of the capital, the Bell and Drum Towers always coexisted with the royal palaces in capital city and was the telling-time center during the Yuan, Ming and Qing dynasties. The ancient charms emanated by the building will last for good.

Qizheng Tower, also called Former Drum Tower, corresponds to the Drum Tower built in Ming Dynasty. The name of Jiugulou Street sprung from the tower. The northern section of this aged street only stretched to the city wall in the past. On the west of the northern section of the street, there was a Yaowang (God of Medicine) Temple which attracted large numbers of worshipers. This street was also called Yaowang Temple Street. At present, the temple was deserted. Only Guangji (Great Charity) Temple (one of the Twin Temples) exists. There are many aged stores and shops and bulky pagoda trees of over 100 years along Jiugulou Street.

房上的铁挂钩是当年店铺挂
幌子用的（街道拓宽，现已
拆除）

The iron hook used to hang the
shop-sign of the store in the
hutong, which was demolished
during the expansion of the
street.

门前的老槐树依然枝繁叶茂
（街道拓宽，老槐树保留下来）
The prosperous aged pagoda
trees in front of the gate. The
original houses were demolished because of the expansion
of the street.

毛主席故居　Former residence of Chairman Mao Zedong

豆腐池胡同　在钟楼北侧，明代称豆腐陈胡同，清讹传为豆腐池。胡同西头有清代太监退养之地宏恩观，东头15号为杨开慧之父杨怀中故宅，毛泽东1918年初次来京曾居于此处，现为东城文物保护单位。

Doufuchi (Pond of Bean Curd) **Hutong**, to the north of Bell Tower, was called Doufuchen (Chen's Bean Curd) Hutong in Ming Dynasty, but the name was changed to Doufuchi by mispronunciation during the Qing Dynasty. At the west end of the hutong, there was a Hong'en (Grand Favor) Temple which used to be the residence of retired eunuchs in Qing Dynasty. The No.15 Courtyard, at the east end of the alley, was the former house of Yang Huaizhong, father of Yang Kaihui. The young Mao Zedong once lived here when he first visited Beijing in 1918. Now, the house has been put under the municipal protection as the key cultural relics.

豆腐池胡同口悬挂的介绍胡同位置、历史的标牌
The board introducing the location and history of Doufuchi Hutong is hung at its entrance.

毛主席旧居院中的老槐树
The aged pagoda tree in the former
residence of Chairman Mao Zedong

胡同中的娘娘庙旧址
The former site of Niangniang
(Goddess) Temple in the hutong

烟袋斜街 在鼓楼大街西侧。元代为行人在什刹海东北岸踩踏出的一条小路，明代设有管理后海一带捕鱼事务的机构，称"打鱼厅斜街"，到清代这条东西长仅二百余米的小胡同中已有古玩、烟具、茶坊、酒肆等小型店铺百余家，人称北城"小大栅栏"。后来这里聚集了多家经营烟具的店铺，"同合盛"、"双盛泰"曾以给慈禧太后通洗烟袋锅而闻名全城。还有一家烟袋铺挂出了一个长1.5米、黑杆金锅红里的大烟袋招徕顾客，因此被称为烟袋斜街。

Yandai (Tobacco Pipe) Slanting Street Located west to the Gulou Street, this slanting street was stamped out by the passersby in the northeast bank of Shichahai Lake during Yuan Dynasty. An administration in charge of fishing affairs was set up here during the Ming Dynasty, so the street was known as Dayuting (Fishing Department) Slanting Street at the time. In the Qing dynasty, along the 200-meter-nearly street were over 1,000 stores of antique and smoking set, tea houses and wine-shops, so it was reputed " Mini Dazhalan Street" in the north city. Later, many stores of smoking sets grouped here, among which Tonghesheng and Shuangshengtai shops were famous for their business of cleaning the smoking set for Empress Dowager Cixi. What's interesting that there was a shop soliciting customers by hanging a 1.5-meter-long tobacco pipe with black body and golden bowl, hence the name of the street.

雨中的烟袋斜街少了往日的喧闹
Yandai Slanting Street in the rain, retreating from former hustles

小石碑胡同 清代称石碑胡同，为银锭桥头繁华的小巷，店铺林立，人流如潮，清晨傍晚商贩云集。

Xiaoshibei (Little Stone Stele) Hutong was called Shibei Hutong in Qing Dynasty. It was a prosperous hutong at the end of Yinding (Silver Ingot) Bridge. The alley was packed with stores and shops and hustling people. Vendors swarmed here in the morning and at dusk.

在鼓楼上北望钟楼
Viewing the Bell Tower from Drum Tower

夜晚的银锭桥旁，后海酒吧灯火通明。　　Brilliantly illuminated pubs beside the Yinding Bridge at the banks of Houhai Lake

雪后钟楼湾胡同
Zhonglouwan (Bell-Tower Cove) Hutong after snow

雪后的银锭桥胡同异常宁静
Yindingqiao (Silver Ingot Bridge) Hutong after the snow in exceptionally tranquil

入夜，什刹海岸边的酒吧流光溢彩，热闹非凡，这里已成为京城夜生活的一个新亮点。

A night scene of uncommonly lively and glaring pubs at the banks of Shichahai Lake, a new feature of night life in Beijing.

小雪后的银锭桥　Yinding Bridge after mild snow

坐冰车是孩子们在冬季最喜欢的游戏
Ice tackle, a favorite game enjoyed by children in winter

什刹海岸边的酒吧吸引着中外游客
Tourists from abroad and at home attracted
by pubs beside the Shichahai Lake

后海南沿街头的夏日夜晚
The night of the southern bank of
Houhai (Rear Sea) Lake in Summer

钟楼东侧的草厂北巷胡同

大新开胡同中一个四合
院的大门，门前的石头
台阶异常宽大。
The front gate of a
Siheyuan in Daxinkai
(Big New-Opening)
Hutong and the excep-
tionally large and broad
stone stairs in front of the
gate.

南官房胡同

在银锭桥南侧，清代称南官府胡同，后改称南官房。官房亦做关防，为正黄旗地界。

Nanguanfang Hutong, to the south of Yinding Bridge, was called Nanguanfu (Southern Local Authorities) Hutong in Qing Dynasty and renamed as Nanguanfang (Southern Official House) later. The "Guanfang" has the same pronunciation with the words " official seal" or " guarding frontier". The area was under the jurisdiction of Zhenghuangqi (Plain Yellow Banner) at the time.

精美的砖雕
Exquisitely carved bricks

三座桥胡同与羊角灯胡同交汇处
The crossing of Sanzuoqiao (Three Bridges) Hutong and YangJiaodeng (Ram's Horn Lamp) Hutong

小雪过后，天空依然阴沉着，清晨的兴华胡同静悄悄。
The sky is still gloomy after a mild snow, while it was very quiet
in Xinghua (Vitalizing China) Hutong in the early morning.

毡子胡同
Zhanzi (Felt) Hutong

藕芽胡同　　在护国寺北侧。昔日每逢护国寺庙会之际，贩买鲜藕、黄、绿豆芽菜的小贩均集中于此胡同中，1911年后得此名。胡同中多为民居，也有退隐官员的豪宅，房顶上的"福""寿"字砖雕和屋檐下的花鸟图案都显示了故主的文化素养。

Ouya (Lotus Rhizome and Bean Sprouts) Hutong is located to the north of Huguo (Defending the Country) Temple. Vendors selling lotus rhizomes, soybean sprouts and mung bean sprouts swarmed in this hutong when the temple fair was held in the past, so the hutong's name came into being after 1911. There were many residents of common people and luxurious mansions of retired high-ranking officials. The brick sculptures with characters of " Fu (happiness)" and " Shou (longevity)" on the roof, as well as design of flowers and various birds under eaves reveal the cultural attainments of the former owners.

左为"寿"字，右为"福"字。
The left is the Chinese characters of "Shou (longevity)" and the right is "Fu (happiness)".

伴随着录音机中悠扬的舞曲，胡同里的少年跳起探戈来有模有样。
Wonderful performance of young Tango dancers in the alley

垂花门的一角被隔到了墙外，油漆斑驳脱落，但精美的镂空雕花依然能让人想像出当年这座院落的豪华。

A part of the tassel gate was kept away outside the wall. Although the paint has come off, the carved flowers still remind the tourists of its past luxury.

护国寺街旁的一个小院
A small yard beside Huguo Temple

百花深处 的名称，据传始自明代万历年间，当年有一对张氏夫妇在此以种菜为业，同时在菜园中栽植牡丹、芍药、荷藕等花木，春夏之交百花竞放，香随风来，菊黄月明之秋，梅红映雪之日，四时风光无限，引得骚人墨客流连忘返，此处遂被称为百花深处。岁月如流，物随时变，到民国时期这狭而长的胡同"两旁都是用碎砖砌的墙，南墙少见日光，薄薄地长着一层绿苔，高处有隐隐的几条蜗牛爬过的银轨，"（摘自老舍《老张的哲学》）百花深处失去树木和百花后，护国寺的西配殿就成了这条胡同的灵魂。在百花深处与护国寺西巷交汇处可见飞檐翘角、庄严肃穆的护国寺西配殿，它使这条胡同更加幽深、古朴。可惜在 2004 年 6 月 20 日凌晨，一场无情的大火将护国寺西配殿化为一片断壁残垣，而今仔细欣赏王文波先生为百花深处留下的护国寺西配殿的倩影，再看看被烈火烧得面目全非的山墙和斗拱，在痛心之余，也让人听到了古建筑保护的红色警报。如果它能对文物保护工作起到警醒作用，也算是不幸中的大幸了。

Baihua Shenchu (Deep in Hundreds of Flowers) It was said that a couple, Mr. and Mrs. Zhang, planted vegetables to make a living during Ming Emperor Wan Li's reign. In the meantime, they grew peony, Chinese herbaceous peony, lotus and other flowers and trees. During the spring and summer, the place was taken over by a riot of flowers, which contended in beauty and fascination and sent off sweet fragrance; in autumn, yellow chrysanthemums and bright moon set each other off beautifully; while in winter, red plum blossomed defiantly in snow. The dissimilar charming in four seasons had attracted an endless flow of celebrities and poets, therefore, the hutong was named Baihua Shenchu. As time goes by, everything changes. As stated in Lao She's novel, *Lao Zhang's Philosophy*, during Republic of China this narrow but long hutong was lined with walls built of broken bricks on both sides; the southern wall was covered with green mosses due to the lack of sunshine, on the top of which there were vague traces of snails. The western attached hall of Huguo Temple turned out to be the soul of the hutong after the death of trees and flowers. People could see the imposing and stately hall with flying eaves and raising angles at the juncture of Baihua Shenchu Hutong and Western Huguo Temple Lane, which intensify the secluded and ancient atmosphere in the hutong. Unfortunately, a ruthless fire reduced the hall to broken walls in the small hours of June 20, 2004. The pretty pictures of the western attached hall of Huguo Temple in Baihua Shenchu taken by Mr.Wang Wenbo makes a poignant contrast with broken walls and arches damaged by the fire, which should remind people of the urgent preservation of ancient buildings. It will be fortunate if the fire can sound the alarm for the protection of cultural relics.

前帽胡同 位于新街口大街西侧，明代开有帽子作坊，故称帽儿胡同。清代按方位分为前、后、中、大、北五条帽儿胡同。此巷在后帽胡同南，因北京习俗北方为上方，所以称前帽胡同。

Qianmao (Front Cap) **Hutong** is situated to the west of Xinjiekou (Opening of New Street) Street. There were cap workshops in Ming Dynasty here, so the hutong was named after them. During the Qing Dynasty, the area boasted 5 hutongs, namely Qianmao (Front Cap), Houmao (Rear Cap), Zhongmao (Middle Cap), Damao (Big Cap) and Beimao (North Cap). This hutong is to the south of Houmao. It was called Qianmao Hutong because the North is regarded as the " up" direction in the customs of Beijing.

后帽胡同 位于前帽胡同之北，故称后帽胡同。

Houmao Hutong is to the north of Qianmao Hutong and so the name came into being.

中帽胡同 因此巷横穿前、后帽胡同，所以叫做中帽胡同。

Zhongmao Hutong   The alley is called Zhongmao Hutong, for it goes through Qianmao Hutong and Houmao Hutong.

兵马司胡同　元世祖忽必烈迁都北京之后，改金代的"警巡院"为"兵马司"，专理捕盗及殴斗等事，明、清两代相沿此称，在内外城设立有东西南北中五个兵马司。西城兵马司设在今丰盛胡同北边，胡同西口正对政协礼堂。"兵马司"其实既无兵也无马，不掌兵权，而相似于今日的公安局。但"兵马司"这个地名，今日算来已有600～800年的历史了。

Bingmasi (Bureau of Troops and Horses) Hutong Kublai Khan, Emperor Shizu of Yuan Dynasty, renamed the " Jingxunyuan (Court of Guarding and Patrolling)" as " Bingmasi" after he moved the capital to Beijing. The authority took charge of arresting of thieves and gangs. Its name was inherited by Ming and Qing dynasties. There established a total of 5 such departments in the four directions inside and outside Beijing city. The one in the western district was set up to the north of today's Fengsheng (Rich) Hutong whose western entrance faces the conference hall of Chinese People's Political Consultative Conference (CPPCC). This authority fulfilled the responsibilities that are similar to those of current public security bureau. It had no army or horses, and did not take control of army, either, although it was so called. This name has a history of 600-800 years.

福绥境 是古都北京内城西北域的一个著名的街道办事处。它辖有中央、市属、区属单位 80 余个，绿树繁花掩映着古老的四合院，高楼广厦立交桥伴随着千年古刹、巍巍白塔，呈现出一派祥和宁静、福寿相绥的胜境景况。历史上的福绥境曾有过悲古的一页，明清之际这里因为有一口水量充沛的苦水井而闻名，地名就叫"苦水井"，清末民初以福禄绥之的寓意将地名改为福绥境，原在胡同 16 号南侧的苦水井已被填埋。

Fusuijing (Land of Happiness and Blessing) is a well-known sub-district office in the northwest of the ancient capital Beijing. There are more than 80 departments belonging to central government, metropolitan government and district government within its administration. Ancient Siheyuans are shrouded among blooming flowers and trees; skyscrapers and overpasses accompany the antique temple of more than 1,000 years and lofty white dagoba, all striking the tourists with the scene of tranquil happiness and coexistence of blessing and longevity. There was a sorrowful chapter in Fusuijing's history. This place was well-known for a well with abundant bitter water in the Ming and Qing dynasties and called "Kushuijing (Bitter Water Well)" at that time. Then, the name was changed to Fusuijing in the end of Qing Dynasty and the beginning of the Republic of China, with the implied meaning of appeasement of happiness and blessing.

秀才胡同 在福绥境北侧。秀才是封建时代科举考试，经过初考合格的人，又称生员。它是读书人进入官员行列的基本条件。秀才通过乡试选取举人，中举后再经过全国考试中进士、点状元而进入官场。明代这里有一个名称奇特的小庙叫秀头庵，据传这里住有一个秀才，很有学问，一生中在这一带培养、教育出许多秀才，但这位满腹经纶的秀才从青年考到老年始终没能考中举人，最后抱恨而终，胡同也留下了秀才之名。后来从南往北三条并列的胡同又被命名为前、中、后秀才胡同（现已拆除）。

Xiucai Hutong is to the north of Fusuijing. *Xiucai* were those skillful writers who had passed the preliminary national examinations in ancient China, also known as *Shengyuan*. This title was the basic qualification for one to become an official in the government. *Xiucai* was selected as *Juren* after he passed the village exams. After that stage, *Juren* would be selected as *Jinshi* only after he passed the national exams, and then be chosen as an official. There was an eerie small temple called Xiutou (Chief of *Xiucai*) Hut in which a talented *Xiucai* lived. He fostered many *Xiucais* during his life time. However, this *Xiucai* of geniuses failed to pass village exams from his youth to old age. Finally, he died with considerable regrets. This Hutong was named after this *Xiucai*. Later, three collateral hutongs from the south to the north were named as Qian (Front) *Xiucai* Hutong, Zhong (Middle) *Xiucai* Hutong and Hou (Rear) *Xiucai* Hutong respectively. It was demolished.

鞍匠胡同 清代阜成门至西直门内为正红旗驻扎之地，这里设有弓匠营、鞍匠营等，分别制造弓箭和马鞍等。民国后改称弓匠和鞍匠胡同，从而留下了清代八旗驻防的历史遗痕。

Anjiang (Craftsman Making Saddle) *Hutong* During Qing Dynasty, the Zhenghongqi (Plain Red Banner) was stationed from Fucheng Gate to Xizhi Gate, so workshops of bow and saddle were set up there, manufacturing bows, arrows and saddles respectively. This area was named as Gongjiang (Craftsman Making Bow) Hutong and Anjiang Hutong in the Republic of China, which preserved the historical traces of the garrisoning of Eight-Banners of the Qing Dynasty.

鞍匠胡同（已拆除）
Anjiang Hutong (It no longer exists)

夕阳中的一座影壁墙。几天之后这里被拆平了。

A shadow wall in the setting sun. Several days later, it was dismantled completely.

新式婚礼吸引着胡同里的大人和孩子前来观看。(1996 年 5 月摄于秀洁胡同，现胡同已拆除)
Grow-ups and children attracted by a fashionable wedding ceremony in Hutong (photo was taken in
May 1996 in Xiujie, or Elegant and Pure, Hutong, which does not exist now).

秋天的小乘巷胡同
Xiaochengxiang (Hinayana Lane) Hutong in autumn

后公用胡同
Hougongyong (Rear Public) Hutong

福寿里雪景
Fushouli (Lane of Happiness
and Longevity) in the snow

武定胡同 在白塔寺南侧，因明代开国功臣郭英被封为武定侯，其后人曾居此而名为武定侯胡同。武定侯郭英的后人郭勋承袭官爵后，管操神机营，后来晋封为翊国公，加太师衔。权相严嵩倒台后，郭勋亦被捕，次年死于狱中。郭勋生前曾刊刻了一部开本很大的《水浒传》，称为武定侯本，是版本学家所注目的《水浒传》重要版本之一。（现已拆除）

Wuding (Martial Stability) **Hutong** is to the south of the Baita (White Dagoba) Temple. Guo Ying, one of the heroic founders of Ming Dynasty was conferred a title Marquis Wuding. His descendants lived here, so the hutong was named after Guo's title. Guo Xun, a descendant of Guo Ying, inherited the rank of nobility and took charge of Divine Skill Division - the troop equipped with guns. Later, he was promoted to be Duck Yiguo and granted as the Taishi (Grand Tutor). Guo Xun was arrested and died in the prison after the powerful prime minister of Yan Song fell from the power. Guo Xun once printed a large-format *Shui Hu Zhuan* (*Outlaws of the Marsh*) called Marquis Wuding's Edition which was one of the prominent versions of *Shui Hu Zhuan*. It attracted the attention of edition experts. The hutong has been demolished.

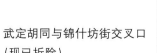

武定胡同与锦什坊街交叉口
（现已拆除）
The crossing of Wuding Hutong and Jinshifang (Fang in Jin's Capital) Street. It no longer exists.

长安街　在元大都时，本是大都城的南部城垣。明初扩建北京城将南部城墙移至今崇文门、正阳门、宣武门一线，原城墙处渐成一条东西方向的大街，但是被长安左门、长安右门及东单牌楼、西单牌楼等分隔成几段。20世纪50年代，位于天安门东西两侧的长安街分别向东西方向拓展到通县和石景山，形成全长近50公里、宽80~120米的百里长街，被誉为京城第一街。20世纪80年代，每当早晚上下班时，这里的自行车流一泻千里，气势恢宏。（摄于1984年6月）

Chang'an (Eternal Peace) Boulevard　The street was once the site of southern wall of the Dadu of Yuan Dynasty. During the expansion of Beijing city in the beginning of Ming Dynasty, the southern wall was extended to the Chongwen Gate, Zhengyang Gate and Xuanwu Gate. The original site developed into an avenue from the east to the west gradually. However, the whole avenue was partitioned into several sections by Left Chang'an Gate, Right Chang'an Gate, Dongdan Archway and Xidan Archway. In the 1950's, the street was expanded on both ends, forming a boulevard stretching from Tongxian County in the east to Shijingshan District in the west. Around 50 kilometers long and 80-120 meters wide, it was reputed as the No.1 Boulevard in China. In the 1980's, the stream of bicycles was exceptionally striking phenomenon during the peak hours in the morning and evening. (This photo was taken in June, 1984)

新文化街 在宣武门内大街西侧，明朝宣宗顺德公主驸马石璟的府第曾在此胡同中，明清之际均称石驸马街。街中的45号是北京158中学（原为国立北平大学女子师范学院，鲁迅先生曾在此校任教），"三·一八"惨案中遇难的刘和珍与杨德群墓在此校园内。1969年为纪念新文化运动的积极倡导者鲁迅，特将此胡同更名为新文化街。

Xinwenhua (New Culture) **Street** is located to the west of Xuanwumennei Street. Shi Jing, husband of Ming Emperor Xuanzong's daughter, Princess Shunde, once lived in this hutong. So it was known as Shifuma (literally, emperor's son-in-law surnamed Shi) during the Ming and Qing dynasties. The No.45 Courtyard on this street is the Beijing No.158 Middle School (it used to be the Woman Normal School of National Beiping University of which Mr. Lu Xun had been a teacher). Liu Hezhen and Yang Dequn, who were both killed in " March 18 Massacre", were buried in the school. The hutong was renamed as Xinwenhua Street in 1969 in memory of Lu Xun, the enthusiastic initiator of the New Culture Movement.

新文化街西口
Western entrance to the Xinwenhua Street

158 中学（原为国立北平大学女子师范学院）的校园依旧保持着昔日的模样
The intact schoolyard of No.158 Middle School on the site of the Woman Normal School of National Beiping University keeps its original shape.

顶银胡同（下）和胡同中一处院落的
西式门楼（上）
Dingyin (Silver Top) Hutong (lower)
and the western style gatehouse (upper)
in this Hutong

大甜水井胡同　Datianshuijing (Big Sweet-Water Well) Hutong

忙里偷闲的修车工（摄于1990年）
Bicycle repairer snatches a little leisure from
his busy work (taken in 1990)

贡院西街的修鞋摊
A shoes repairing stall in West Gongyuan
(site of imperial examinations) Street

阴历大年三十的午夜十二点，京城里烟花飞舞，爆竹齐鸣，一派红红火火、除旧迎新的景象。（摄于1993年阴历大年三十的午夜）

At 12 pm in the last day of lunar year, the flying fireworks and screaming firecrackers celebrated the advent of a new year. (taken at midnight of the last day of the lunar year in 1993)

老城、皇城、新城——见证着北京的发展
Old city, royal city and new city —— witnesses to the developments of Beijing

图书在版编目（CIP）数据

胡同的记忆／杨茵 旅舜编. — 北京：中国民族摄影艺术出版社，2005.12
ISBN 7-80069-709-6

Ⅰ.胡... Ⅱ.杨... Ⅲ.①城市道路－北京市－图集 ②民居－北京市－图集
Ⅳ.K921-64

中国版本图书馆 CIP 数据核字（2005）第 127847 号

策　　划：旅　舜	Planner: Lü Shun
杨　茵	Yang Yin
责任编辑：鲁宝春	Managing Editor: Lu Baochun
摄　　影：王文波	Photographer: Wang Wenbo
撰　　文：刘建斌	Writer: Liu Jianbin
装帧设计：赵鸿生	Designer: Zhao Hongsheng

《胡同的记忆》摄影画册
中国民族摄影艺术出版社　出版
北京华天旅游国际广告公司　承制
开本：　787mm × 1092mm　1/12
印张：　12
印数：　1-3,000
版次：2006 年 1 月第一版第一次印刷
书号：ISBN 7-80069-709-6/J.433
+8610-67018834
0012000

Recollections of Hutong
Published by China Nationality Art Photograph Publishing House
Produced by Beijing Huatian International Tourism Advertising Co.
Format:　787mm × 1092mm　1/12
Printed Sheet:　12
Impression:　3,000
Printed Order: First Impressions & First Edition in January, 2006
www. jdbybook.com
www. 旅游图书.cn